Philosophy and the teacher

edited by
D. I. Lloyd
Principal Lecturer in Education
Stockwell College of Education

Routledge & Kegan Paul
London and New York

First published in 1976
by Routledge & Kegan Paul Ltd
11 New Fetter Lane, London EC4P 4EE
Published in the USA by
Routledge and Kegan Paul Inc.
in association with Methuen Inc.
29 West 35th Street, New York NY 10001
Reprinted in 1978, 1979, 1983 and 1986
Set in IBM Press Roman by
Express Litho Service (Oxford)
and printed in Great Britain by
Redwood Burn Ltd
Trowbridge, Wiltshire
© Routledge & Kegan Paul Ltd 1976

ISBN 0 7100 8282 7 (C)
ISBN 0 7100 8288 6 (P)

The Students Library of Education has been designed to meet the needs of students of Education at Colleges of Education and at University Institutes and Departments. It will also be valuable for practising teachers and educationists. The series takes full account of the latest developments in teacher-training and of new methods and approaches in education. Separate volumes will provide authoritative and up-to-date accounts of the topics within the major fields of sociology, philosophy and history of education, educational psychology, and method. Care has been taken that specialist topics are treated lucidly and usefully for the non-specialist reader. Altogether, the Students Library of Education will provide a comprehensive introduction and guide to anyone concerned with the study of education, and with educational theory and practice.

Most books in philosophy of education to date are suitable for students who are beginning to specialise in the subject. There has been very little written of a simple, introductory sort for those with no previous experience of the subject at all. This collection of papers, therefore, carefully constructed by a team of lecturers in philosophy of education at Stockwell College of Education, is designed to meet a real need. It is the product of their experience over several years of putting on elementary courses in philosophy of education to students for the Teacher's Certificate. The topics selected and the level of presentation have been found suitable for students at this elementary stage. Their hope is that this record of past endeavours will be of help to other students and lecturers in the same position.

R. S. PETERS

Contents

Contents

Acknowledgments

The editor and contributors would like to thank Professor R. S. Peters for his encouragement and advice; Mr. John Elwell who read the manuscript and made some helpful suggestions; and last, and by no means least, the typists.

Introduction

When students first begin to study philosophy they do not find it easy. Often they find it more difficult than other subjects. The aim of these essays has not been to break new ground in educational philosophy but to help students over their first acquaintance with it.

What then is philosophy? We probably cannot get very far in answering this until we have actually done some philosophy (imagine trying to describe music to someone who had never heard any!). However, it may help if we contrast the activity of the philosopher with that of the astronomer or psychologist. The two latter acquire what is called empirical knowledge — that is, knowledge derived from observation, about the stars and planets or the reasons why people behave as they do. Their findings can be proved or disproved by the evidence that our senses provide. The philosopher, on the other hand, is not concerned with what people observe but with the ideas (concepts) that they employ, the assumptions they make and the arguments they advance about these observations. That is why we call philosophy a *conceptual* activity. In education, for example, the philosopher will ask the psychologist what he means by 'reading'. Does it mean being able to pronounce words in the book correctly or does it mean that you should be able to understand them as well? If this idea is not made clear beforehand the psychologist may look for the wrong evidence and end up with what is not relevant. Philosophy is very important for getting one's ideas clear and should be seen as an ally of empirical study and not its enemy. Empirical enquiry itself is essential in our search for knowledge, which is all the more reason why clarity about its aims are necessary. Sometimes the philosopher finds there is confusion in the minds of those engaged in such enquiry and is critical of them. For example, the findings of some psychological research which is regarded as being of value in our study of human beings is challenged in Chapter 3. Here the ideas the researcher has of human nature seem to be so confused that his conclusions if accepted could be positively harmful.

1

Introduction

Throughout we have tried to make clear what arguments people have used in supporting their views and we have tried, as philosophers should, to be fair and sympathetic to them. We hope that in reading the chapters you will begin to learn how to think philosophically and to apply your thinking to other areas of education. It is important to learn to attend closely to the person's argument and to question its assumptions, as well as the way he arrives at his conclusions. To enable you to consider other points of view there are references at the end of each chapter to other writings. The exercise of comparing two opposing views on one topic will take you a long way towards being able to develop philosophical arguments of your own. Philosophy, then, is invaluable in that it enables those involved in education to consider the ideas and arguments behind their classroom practice and the innovations they may consider producing. This is why we speak of philosophy as being conceptual rather than empirical in character, but none the less relevant to education.

Not everyone sees the value of philosophy in the way that has been described. Some are even hostile to the subject for a number of reasons. Perhaps three of these reasons are worth considering.

1 Many feel that philosophical reasoning is no more than words and yet more words. It is so concerned with the verbal that it is not related to the practical. As was shown above, by its very nature philosophy steps back from the scene to have a clear view. In so doing it can take too long a step and the detail of the picture is lost. The same mistake can be made by psychology and sociology. They may get interested in areas of human experience which have no relevance to education. In such cases they no longer can be 'studies of education'. But the alternative of taking no step back at all, but instead to get on with the job of teaching is no better. Is it not important to ask what job? Doing something for the sake of it, no matter what it is, can bring about a good deal of harm that we will come to regret. The concrete jungles that the town planners have produced for us are all too real. Much organisation and money was devoted to building them, but a little more thought beforehand might have prevented the disasters that have occurred. Similarly, in education, the adoption of new forms of organisation like the integrated day, new subjects on the primary curriculum or new tasks the teacher has been asked to take upon himself, like counselling – all these are practical in nature, too, but their wholesale adoption, without reflection, may produce more harm than good.

2 Sometimes the hostility towards philosophy is stronger. Philosophy is seen to be destructive, verbally tearing into shreds what people have accepted, valued and perhaps worked for, for a long time. For example, Socrates, the father of philosophy, was put to death for challenging the moral views of his contemporaries. Yet what he was

doing was being critical of the reason why they held their views. He showed that they behaved as they did not because they thought what they were doing was right, but because it was the 'done thing'. Their morality was a matter of mere habit and, as we know, habits can be good or bad. Socrates' so-called 'destructiveness' was intended to create an honest and thoughtful morality. In education, Rousseau initiated reforms because he was critical of existing thought and practice. And if sometimes the views of philosophers amount to no more than personal prejudice it is they who are at fault and not philosophy. They are, at that time, doing bad philosophy, for it is the mark of the good philosopher that he follows an argument where it leads. He must neither rush to conclusions nor shy away from the demands of logic just because he finds them unpalatable. The student of education who does likewise will be following a tradition of thinkers who have helped to advance our understanding of educational issues and practice.

3   Finally, philosophy is seen as a cold and rational activity devoid of warmth and emotion. Sometimes the philosopher displays a lack of involvement, appears dispassionate and uncommitted in the presence of differing points of view. He does this not because he has no emotions but because he may feel that some emotions get in the way of his activity. He is not without emotion but tries to ensure that he has the appropriate one. For example, he should fight for impartiality. He should be enthusiastic about his study. He finds his work stimulating, emotionally enriching and intellectually intriguing in itself, but also for the light it throws on practical matters such as education. We hope that the chapters in this book will help readers to find it so.

The first chapter by D. S. Wringe, 'The teacher's task', looks at the nature and scope of teaching. This essay is timely in view of the increasing recommendations to extend the already demanding responsibilities of the teacher. Of the traditional function of the teacher — namely, to teach the child something — the remark that what he is doing is really indoctrinating his pupils is common as rain. The idea is that any communication of thought or fact, by virtue of its selection, is an imposition on free thinking. However, M. A. B. Degenhardt's chapter 2 examines various views of indoctrination and offers an account of the way to minimise indoctrination by maximising education. Of course, whether we are to adopt such a method of teaching depends on how we see the person we are teaching. Do we regard him as someone who needs to be manipulated like a complicated machine, or some interesting animal who needs conditioning? D. I. Lloyd (chapter 3) compares Man with three models, machine, plant and animal, in trying to elicit what is special about him. His conclusion is that man has something that these lack, understanding.

In the six chapters which follow these, the writers concentrate on education and the curriculum. P. J. Higginbotham, in 'Aims of education' (chapter 4), presents considerations that must be borne in mind if we are to have clear and justifiable views in education. She examines separately the notion of education and that of aims, with a conviction that aimlessness is one of the common weaknesses in teaching. Perhaps the most fundamental question that can be asked is whether anything can be taught. Can there be knowledge? At a time when people question whether we can be certain of anything, some examination of this question is necessary, for the foundations of education are being threatened. In chapter 5 this age-old argument is considered, and the writer attempts to show that knowledge must exist. Chapter 6, 'Forms of knowledge', characterises the nature of this knowledge. Knowledge is shown to be of different kinds. Rather than deal cursorily with various branches of knowledge, the chapter concerns itself with one, namely, historical knowledge. The writer draws on the now familiar 'forms of knowledge' view, associated with Professor P. H. Hirst, but is also critical of that point of view in certain respects.

It is the curriculum which is the means of conveying education in school. D. S. Wringe continues her contribution (chapter 7) by showing how the various forms of knowledge are related to the planning of the curriculum. She looks particularly at the current and popular idea of 'integration' and its relation to curriculum planning and also at the idea of the common curriculum.

Two familiar traditions in education, each with its particular curriculum have been the traditional and the progressive. D. I. Lloyd (chapter 8) looks briefly at these two educational philosophies. He maintains that these past as well as present traditions in education differ not only in emphasis but also about the matter and manner of education; and that within those traditions there is considerable variation, so that a teacher's mere statement of allegiance to one or the other still leaves one in doubt as to what his views are. A concern for creativity is a feature of many progressive curricula; but M. A. B. Degenhardt (chapter 9) argues that traditional education also has much to teach us about how to educate for creativity.

The final two chapters are concerned with the social climate and conditions in which education takes place. All human activities are of a social kind and no introductory book on education could justifiably omit this important area. Just two aspects have been taken – freedom and authority. F. M. Berenson, on 'Freedom' (chapter 10), argues that the best way to enable children to enjoy freedom is to provide them with a planned experience. Letting them get on by themselves will not enable that to take place. A familiar cry these days is that we are oppressed by those in authority. Behind this cry is seen the implicit desire to obliterate authority in general. Finally, D. H. Cleife (chapter 11) claims that to try to remove authority from the human scene is to breed confusion. He shows that authority is a logical necessity in any society. He sees these cries as desires to participate in matters of decision and not to be ignored. He argues no less strongly that the teacher must remain as an authority if education is to continue.

In these essays we have only considered selected educational topics and where we have drawn conclusions we hope that readers will not regard them as final. We will have succeeded in our aims if we stimulate readers to think, discuss and read more about educational philosophy.

Chapter one

The teacher's task

D.S.Wringe

If you are among those who have decided to take up teaching as a career you will already have some idea of what it is like to stand in front of a class. The picture you have, however, will depend on your own school experience and this may be rather different from the situation you are preparing to meet. Indeed you may discover as a result of further visits or reading, that many of the things which teachers do, or are encouraged to do nowadays, are very different from what you had expected. Soon, like them, you may be urged to adopt an unfamiliar role. Perhaps it will be suggested that you should become a 'manager' of resources — a kind of technological whizz-kid laden with film projectors, tape recorders, teaching machines and the rest of the latest gadgetry. Alternatively, you may be encouraged to see yourself as a kind of educational shepherd guiding your pupils lovingly along the paths of learning and discovery while lending an ever-ready ear to their difficulties and problems. Some will doubtless propose that you join forces with local social workers and take up home visiting while others will attempt to persuade you to pay less attention to teaching children and devote your energies to teaching parents instead. Given this profusion of ideas about how teachers should see their job I am going to begin the discussion of the teacher's task by looking into the nature of teaching itself.

The nature of teaching

The first thing I shall do is to try to sort out what it means to teach somebody. In other words, I want to try to establish the kind of thing a person would have to be doing if it was in any way appropriate to describe him as teaching. Having clarified what is implied when we describe someone as teaching we can then go on to see if some of the classroom approaches currently in favour really are forms of teaching, and if so whether they provide more fruitful alternatives to the traditional ones.

One of the first things to note is that a statement like 'Miss Smith is teaching 3X maths this term' can be taken in two ways. It may mean that she is trying to get her pupils to learn maths even though she is failing hopelessly. On the other hand it may mean that her methods are succeeding so that one of 3X might say, 'I've had dozens of maths teachers but only Miss Smith taught me anything.' What is important then about Miss Smith's teaching is that she not only intends her pupils to learn some maths; they really do learn some.

The connection between learning and teaching, however, is complicated because not all learning is the result of someone's teaching. Members of 3X had no doubt learnt to distract their various teachers' attention in a number of time-honoured ways. Some, no doubt, had originally learnt how to do this by imitating the ring-leaders in the class. They did not need to be taught.

Sometimes, then, we try to teach people without success; sometimes they learn things which no one actually sets out to teach them. This does not mean, however, that teachers like Miss Smith and her colleagues should stop trying to teach their pupils, nor that they should rely on their learning certain important things in other ways. In other words, it is no accident that over the centuries teachers have tried to get pupils to learn things by teaching them. In general we *do* learn things as a result of being taught and that is why teachers who wish us to learn attempt to get us to do this by teaching us.

Another reason why it matters what teachers do in the classroom is because we regard it as highly desirable that children should learn certain things. As educators, teachers have definite views about what these things are, and why they are important. All this will be discussed more fully in chapter 4. It is clear for the moment, however, that we do want pupils to be able to learn to read and perform mathematical operations, for example, to speak French, to be able to swim, to know some science or some history, and so on. If you agree that learning things like this *is* important then it will also be clear why people make serious attempts to teach them. But what is it exactly to make such an attempt? This brings us now to the heart of the matter. What sort of things might a teacher do which would justify his pupils' claim that he had taught them? Surely he would have had to set about the task in a particular way. For example, if a teacher really wanted his pupils to learn to swim, he could not possibly think it adequate simply to show them the way to the nearest swimming pool. Similarly, if he wanted them to learn to read he could not think it enough just to provide them with books. Indeed, we can make similar points about each of the achievements referred to above. What is missing in each case is some attempt to make explicit for the pupil exactly what is involved in being able to swim, to read and so on.

Now let us imagine a teacher who did want to make it as clear as possible to his pupils how to master a particular achievement. How might he set about it? Well, he might use one or more of the following devices: he might tell his pupils certain things, give them explanations and demonstrations, set them appropriate tasks and comment on their efforts to perform them, answer their questions or ask them questions. In doing these things he would be doing everything he possibly could in order to get his pupils to learn. If you doubt this, ask yourself if it is possible to imagine anything of a fundamentally different kind which he *could* do in order to make achievements like those of swimming, reading and so on available to them. If you find that this is indeed impossible to imagine then you will understand the basis on which activities like those listed above – which many would regard as teaching activities, properly so called – are distinguished from other things which teachers sometimes have to do in the course of their day's work. For example, teachers might have to look up the way to the swimming baths or to order a set of reading books but these are not *themselves* teaching activities.

Now teachers often have to choose their teaching activities with a number of considerations in mind. In theory, perhaps, the more explicit it is made to the pupil what he is intended to learn, the more likely he is to learn it. Indeed, programmed learning techniques are based on this assumption. In practice, however, methods which take into account the pupil's initial lack of interest are sometimes more likely to succeed, even though they are a more roundabout way of presenting what is to be learnt.

It is undoubtedly true that some pupils do resist attempts to get them to learn things which seem to them to have nothing to do with their own inclinations and purposes. Think of the now notorious television class in 'Please Sir!' Some teachers think that reluctant learners like these would be more responsive if they were allowed to take the initiative and organise their own learning. Teachers who share this view concentrate on managing situations so that resources for learning are available as required by pupils. In this situation teachers see their task as making it *possible* for pupils to encounter or discover things of educational importance which other more directive teachers try to *ensure* that they come to grips with.

Now it is obviously important for teachers to choose methods which enable pupils to attend willingly to what they are trying to teach. There is a danger, however, that too much emphasis may be placed on gaining pupils' interest and co-operation and that methods which are connected in a much more intimate way with what it is intended to teach may be rejected as old-fashioned, boring or unimaginative.

As well as the pupil's attitude to learning, a second factor which teachers also have to take into account when they choose their methods is the level of the pupil's understanding. If you have ever tried to teach an intelligent two-year-old, for example, to name the colours of his toys correctly you will almost certainly have met with a notable lack of success — even when the child can name the toys correctly and pick out other attributes such as size and shape. This would be true whatever strategies you might have adopted for grouping similar toys of different colours or different toys of the same colours. In this situation no amount of telling, explaining and so on seems to work. Nevertheless, the child learns the names of the colours eventually and generally does this without any very deliberately worked out strategies. Indeed, it might be argued by psychologists that too much structured teaching of the sort described is at best useless, at worst actually harmful, when teaching children basic concepts like colour. On the other hand, try asking yourself whether children could learn such concepts at all if there were no coloured objects in the environment and no conversation between adults involving references to them. The point of the example is to show how, in the earliest stages of education, teachers can only do things like provide the conditions which are of vital importance if children are to learn certain fundamental concepts. They cannot *ensure* that children will learn concepts like these at any particular point in time and they certainly cannot rely on central teaching activities like 'telling them the facts'. All they can do, it seems, is to provide an appropriate environment and plenty of discussion about it.

Two arguments have so far been advanced. First, that teaching activities are those which involve deliberate attempts to make explicit what is involved in learning certain things. Second, that the nature of such attempts is determined partly by what it is the teacher wishes to make explicit, partly by the attitudes of his pupils and partly by the level of their conceptual development.

Another important point was made earlier — namely that teachers as educators have a characteristic attitude towards their subject matter. They feel that it is something worth passing on to their pupils. It is also because they are educators that teachers see their pupils in a certain light. For this reason methods which might be effective ways of teaching but which involve children in experiencing pain or serious discomfort are ruled out as inappropriate. Even if it was discovered that pupils learnt best when ravenously hungry, for example, it would still not be on the cards for teachers to deprive them of their lunch.

It is also because they are educators that teachers are required to 'teach' rather than 'condition' or 'brainwash' their pupils. They must, that is, use methods which make it possible for their pupils to achieve some understanding of what they are learning. Some would hold that with very young, or with severely subnormal, children this is impossible, and that the most which can be achieved is the shaping of behaviour in certain ways. But again, you must ask yourself whether you think pupils *could* develop any understanding of the routines their teachers get them to perform unless attempts were made to explain these. In other words, to adopt methods which cannot foster understanding is to prejudge the issue in an important way.

To sum up this section so far, then, some attempt has been made to clarify the *nature* of teaching by seeing the kind of activities which teaching, at least in an educational institution, embraces. But three important areas remain for discussion. Each of these affects the *scope* of the teacher's task — that is, in what kinds of situation and for what kinds of reasons it might be appropriate for teachers to engage in activities *other* than teaching activities pure and simple. These problems will be explored in the following section.

The scope of teaching

In the previous section some attempt was made to see what teaching entails and how teaching activities in the classroom are different from non-teaching activities. But when it comes to deciding what activities teachers ought actually to engage in, whether inside or outside the classroom, it is possible to think of at least three areas of contemporary debate which make us look again at the rather tidy assumption that the teacher's task is to teach his pupils.

First, there are teachers who are more or less clear what teaching consists in. Furthermore, they agree that their main job *is* to teach the pupils in their charge. They understand that they have to discover among other things their pupils' attitudes to learning. What they are not clear about, however, is how far they ought to go in diagnosing attitudes which are hostile to education, as they see it, and in promoting attitudes which make their task as educators easier.

In other words, is it reasonable, some teachers are asking, to visit pupils' homes or even teach pupils' parents in order to make pupils more receptive? If these activities are to be justified is it because they can be seen as a kind of necessary spadework which teachers have to put in before they can begin the real work of teaching? I shall return to this presently.

Second, some teachers think that their first duty, or at least the school's first duty, is to see that the child's most basic needs, for example his physical welfare, are attended to before his educational needs are catered for. Thus in deprived areas especially, where pupils are poorly housed and fed, it is argued that teachers can play an important part in looking after children's general welfare as well as in educating them. This would be a different reason why some people would argue for stronger home—school links. In other words they would see the teacher's work consisting, at least in part, of activities generally undertaken by social workers. I shall consider presently how appropriate this conception of the teacher's task is.

Third, some teachers are very conscious of the fact that their teaching does not take place in a vacuum. For them it is the long-term effects of their interaction with their pupils, or the *totality* of the experiences the latter receive within the educational institution and the *validity* of these which concern them as educators. Such teachers believe that education is to be understood as far more than simply a list of achievements like reading, swimming, speaking French and so on. They believe that the educator is marked out by his concern with the over-all development of his pupils as persons. Granted this, some teachers would go on to argue that activities associated with promoting this development cannot be delegated to other professional agencies. For them education and self-realisation are inextricably connected and this would lead them to challenge the appropriateness of certain activities being undertaken by school counsellors, for example. Furthermore, for some, enabling pupils to establish good personal relationships is an important educational aim, while others would claim that pupils cannot be educated at all (as opposed to being merely taught) unless good relationships exist between teachers and pupils. They would, therefore, regard the fostering of such relationships as an activity which they ought to undertake. In so far as participation in various extra-curricular activities facilitated this, then some would think that here is another case where teachers should be prepared to extend their activities beyond those of teaching pure and simple.

It is now hoped to proceed by examining the three specific areas of home—school links, counselling and the notion of self-realisation, and personal relationships in education. In so doing it is hoped to clarify ways in which teachers as educators might try to sort out the kinds of reason which would seem to justify, or even to necessitate, some extension of their activities beyond those of teaching in the classroom. At the same time the kinds of reason which would make them disinclined to delegate certain of their activities to other professional agencies will be explored.

Home—school links

Obviously if parents and teachers work together at the task of educating a child his education is likely to be more successful. You can see that this kind of co-operation is particularly important where the conditions in the home militate against his doing well in school. Any child is at a disadvantage who comes from a home where material conditions are poor, where language and discipline are radically different from that experienced in the school, where family relationships are poor and where parents are unfavourably disposed towards educational institutions and those who teach in them. A child in this situation gets off to a poor start in the early years of life, is already behind when he begins school, and is less able to benefit from being there. Not only are his parents' attitudes towards school unhelpful; often his teachers' attitudes towards him leave much to be desired.

In the face of these difficulties some educationists have been moved to ask the following questions.

'Might not parents be re-educated to help them to give their children a better start in life?'

'Might not attempts be made to involve them more in school activities, or to help them to see the point of modern approaches?'

'Might not teachers improve their diagnosis of children's difficulties if they visited the home and established informal contact with their parents?'

Some of the answers given to these questions raise a number of difficulties. You will have noticed that I have already distinguished proposals dealing with children's educational needs from those which are concerned with their more general welfare. Perhaps you are inclined to sympathise with teachers who think that the plight of some children is so extreme that it is appropriate to describe the school's most important function as that of detecting and preventing hardship of every kind (Goodacre, *Home and School,* p. 35). If this is so, then you ought perhaps to ask whether it is not possible to sympathise with the plight of children in severe distress without at the same time feeling that *teachers* are necessarily the right people to diagnose and remedy their hardship. Teachers, after all, scarcely possess the expertise which is often required to find adequate solutions to the variety of problems encountered, nor do they have contacts with the appropriate range of specialist helpers such as social workers, health visitors and so on. Then again, teachers are in a position of authority over the children they teach because of their expert knowledge in certain areas. Would they necessarily have — indeed *should* they have — any similar authority over children's parents?

Again, imagine how difficult it might be for teachers who had become closely concerned with the circumstances which prevented their pupils from performing well in school to form objective judgments about their achievements. Yet such judgments are part and parcel of getting children to master the kind of educational attainments teachers are essentially concerned with. If Miss Smith in our earlier example had become too involved with the causes of 3X's behaviour she might have found herself too busy justifying their low level of achievement to think of ways of enabling them to progress beyond this.

Finally, you may be wondering who would carry out the teacher's normal function of teaching if teachers themselves moved over to perform a rather different kind of social service.

I shall now turn to consider those proposals which are concerned more specifically with pupils' educational well-being. As well as suggestions designed to help children while they are still at school, these include attempts to put parents in a position to understand and provide the kind of environment which is best during the early years of childhood.

It is easy to see how much more parents would be likely to give their support and encouragement if they really did see the point of what schools were trying to do. But efforts to involve parents are very time-consuming. This being so, we can evaluate activities designed to bring about parental involvement according to their probable effectiveness and the demands they make on teachers' time. Look at it like this. Somebody might argue that pupils do not make any real progress unless teachers take steps to see that their parents understand what they spend their time doing in school. But such a person would have to admit that the same pupils could hardly make any progress at all unless teachers spent a considerable amount of time teaching them.

Possibly, too, there are other ways in which teachers might spend their time which would result in greater educational benefits for their pupils. Miss Smith's colleagues, for example, might be better off devising more effective methods of teaching maths to 3X than in getting to know their parents, particularly if they do not hit it off with them. Thus plans to involve parents in their children's education must be compared not only amongst themselves but also with other strategies available to the teacher.

There are finally the suggestions for helping pupils to benefit from the educational system before they become the responsibility of any particular school or group of teachers. Here, it seems, some teachers *do* have the expertise needed to help parents but they do not seem to have the corresponding responsibilities. You might feel inclined to say that although this is not the job of the individual school or teachers, local authorities ought to provide a service of this kind and employ teachers to provide tuition for parents.

Pastoral care and counselling

I said in the introduction to this chapter that many teachers are puzzled to know just how far they should go in pursuing their concern for the pupil beyond their encounters with him in particular lessons. This concern is reflected in the present debate in secondary schools, at any rate, about the best way to provide pastoral care in school. Most teachers would admit that those pupils in a class like 3X whose behaviour leads them to be diagnosed as severely disturbed or maladjusted need a special form of help. But if we considered *all* the pupils in the

13

class we should probably also find some who were unhappy or anxious from time to time. Their distress might be due to problems outside the school, although it affected their progress adversely. Then again 3X might contain pupils whose problems resulted from a programme of education ill-suited to their needs. At the same time there would doubtless be a large contingent who, while they had no particular problems, would clearly benefit if somebody took an interest in their all-round development.

In this situation we have to ask whether teachers ought to be concerned with their pupils' general progress. Perhaps school counsellors should be appointed to work more closely with individuals. Many teachers, however, regard the appointment of counsellors as a threat to their traditional kind of role. If pupils can discuss with counsellors problems arising out of their school work then it may seem to teachers that they are in effect able to sidestep their authority. Second, teachers may question whether counsellors can know individuals well enough to advise them and even whether they are qualified to do so on educational matters. Moreover teachers would defend their own contribution to pastoral care not simply on the grounds that they are conveniently placed to be of help. Rather they would say their view of what education is about inevitably involves them in taking an all-round interest in their pupils.

Let us continue then by considering the teacher's role in relation to three kinds of situation. In the first case it would seem teachers are not equipped to do more than refer severely maladjusted or disturbed pupils to specialised agencies. In doing so they are taking the initiative in helping pupils to return to a state of mind in which education becomes for them a realistic possibility.

But whose responsibility ought it to be to deal with those pupils who experience unhappiness, worry or anxiety in relation to fairly specific personal problems such as failure to get on with their parents, to make friends or to fit in at school? You might think that it is for the discussion of such problems as these that counsellors are appointed. Interestingly, though, counsellors themselves appear to feel that their work ought not to be confined to dealing with pupils' existing problems any more than with treating severely maladjusted pupils. Rather they seem to take the view that their job relates to the needs of *all* pupils.

Counsellors, then, believe that they ought to build up over the years the kind of relationship which enables pupils to deal with their lives in such a way that crises are avoided. They hope to enable pupils to answer questions like 'What sort of person am I?' or 'What do I want to make of myself?' This they try to do partly by helping pupils to make an appropriate choice of career. But this choice itself arises naturally out of past choices made in relation to educational opportunities available — and pupils' growing awareness of their own abilities and interests.

All this seems to indicate a down-to-earth and enlightened approach to pupils' problems. Granted this, why should some teachers still regard the appointment of counsellors with suspicion? In order to understand the point of their objection we need to look again at the questions which counsellors claim to be helping children to answer. The fact is that to encourage pupils to ask themselves too early on in their educational career what kind of person they really are is to ignore the important fact that it is education which makes different kinds of 'self' possible at all. In other words most of the things we are we learn to be, and many of the most worthwhile of these, we learn in school. More important then than helping a class like 3X to discover what they are able to do, or are interested in doing, at this moment is the job of making it possible for them to do, and be interested in doing, a greater number of things. The best way of achieving this is not usually by talking to pupils *about* this or that activity but by getting them to participate with success and enjoyment. This is essentially the teacher's job. Thus it is the teacher who communicates the kind of understanding of the world mathematics and science give us, for example, as compared with a love of and concern for the past, or a desire to contribute creatively to one's environment. Indeed it will be argued in chapter 6 that each fundamentally distinct and important form of knowledge contributes the possibility of a different kind of awareness, of different attitudes and values.

For this reason it would be worrying if it became established that the best way to see that pupils develop their potential is to provide them with counsellors to help them form realistic assessments of their abilities, attitudes and aspirations. Similarly suggestions that counsellors with their detailed knowledge of pupils' difficulties, interests, future prospects and so on ought to have a say in deciding what pupils will be taught in school are sensible only up to a certain point. In other words sufficient attention must also be paid to the arguments which *teachers* advance about what it is worthwhile for pupils to learn in the long run. That is to say the curriculum should, in the end, be planned not by counsellors but by teachers!

This point needs developing further. Let us consider the second question which counsellors are interested in helping pupils to answer: 'What do I want to make of my life?', and the practical question which follows from this 'What course shall I follow in school?' Here I would argue that being able to answer these questions at all depends on how far one already understands what a particular form of education amounts to, not just in terms of the job of work it enables one to obtain on leaving school, but also in terms of the way in which one sees one's chosen occupation and the different ways of life which are open to one as a result, in part, of the career one chooses. Some people would argue that the study of subjects like literature, history and religion are particularly important in helping us to settle questions like 'What do I want to make of my life?' since through them different possibilities are opened up for us to consider. Seen in this light subjects such as these are just as 'relevant' to pupils who really are (or should perhaps be) asking this kind of question as courses in catering or commerce which presuppose that pupils have *already* made major decisions about their future lives.

It is for this reason that many teachers would press for the inclusion of, for example, literary, historical and religious studies throughout the pupil's school career and would postpone for as long as possible choices which might eliminate them from the pupil's timetable. Counsellors, on the other hand, with their emphasis on education as a source of job qualification, often favour pupils' choosing fairly early on between courses which are 'outward looking' and designed to lead them easily into jobs of work which exist, and are known by the counsellors to exist in the world beyond the classroom.

I have stressed so far the ways in which the aims of counsellors and the aims of teachers might be seen as conflicting. They might, however, be seen as playing complementary roles in the following way. Teachers, it might be claimed, are primarily concerned to establish the general conditions which make it possible for pupils to make any choices at all about their future. Counsellors on the other hand provide opportunities for individuals to sit down and weigh up the possibilities which exist for them personally in order to make wise choices in their own particular circumstances. Whether it is best to arrange for the provision of this kind of opportunity for pupils by employing counsellors in secondary schools or whether this might be arranged in other ways is, of course, a further question.

Teaching and personal relationships

I said earlier on that many teachers feel that all pupils would benefit from the opportunity to form a relationship with an adult with whom they can discuss their hopes, fears, ambitions and so on. They feel however that to attempt to institutionalise something like personal relationships by making specific arrangements for pastoral care is to miss the important point that these are necessarily informal and spontaneous. We simply cannot guarantee to like or to feel sympathetic towards every pupil in the class. But it is because personal relationships are a very important part of human existence that some teachers attach a great deal of importance to these, and even rank them as *more* important than anything which they actually teach. Not only that, they are inclined to believe that unless a certain kind of relationship exists between the teacher and his pupils, the interaction between them is unlikely to be genuinely educational.

Now however much you might agree about the importance of forming good personal relationships in life generally you might nevertheless
be rather alarmed if you met a teacher who asserted that this indeed
was his *sole* aim in the classroom. As I have said, he might find it
extremely difficult to establish an informal relationship with each
member of the class. More than this however, personal relationships
arise in a context – out of a shared enthusiasm for a subject, for
example. So a teacher who thought he could set about forming them in
a vacuum would be mistaken. In any case he would be under an obligation to show that the formation of personal relationships is more
important than anything else we *might* aim at in education, such as
respect for the countryside, or a sense of civil responsibility.

Of course it might be argued that in his concern to have good
personal relationships with his pupils the teacher really saw himself as
carrying out pupils' moral education, since he might think that it is
within the context of personal relationships that we perform moral
actions, display moral attitudes and so on. But if this is so, then his
view of what moral education actually consists in is certainly very
sketchy. He would be relying on teaching morality by example rather
than by any discussion of what moral decisions are and what important
moral principles we are guided by when we make them. Of course he
might be right in thinking that one of the best ways of showing pupils
that they really *are* respected as individuals with a point of view of their
own is for their teachers to make it clear to them that they do know
them and have some idea of their particular outlook. Teachers who
treat their pupils with the purely formal respect required of them in
their professional role risk having their disinterested treatment mistaken
for treatment marked by lack of interest. On the other hand teachers
who are genuinely interested in and concerned with their pupils are
seen to operate the principle of respect for persons in more than an
empty formal way.

Finally, some teachers might have a rather different kind of reason
for thinking that the formation of good personal relationships with
pupils is central to education. Such a teacher might think that the best
way of conveying to others the significance of being educated is to
allow them to see from time to time the kind of person he is, over and
above being someone who is employed to do a particular job of work.
Thus he might regard participation in voluntary extra-curricular activities as an important aspect of his work as an educator. Of course if
pupils came to share his values, interests and so on, some might claim
that he had come to exercise an undue influence over them. For
them the plight of Miss Jean Brodie's 'girls' highlights the most
sinister possibilities inherent in the teaching situation. Others however would maintain that if teachers make any impact at all on
their pupils which endures after they have slammed their desk lids

shut for the last time it is because they have made some kind of impression as a person which goes beyond the impact they have made simply in their capacity as teachers of a particular subject.

Conclusion

I said at the beginning of the chapter that my intention was to try to make clearer the teacher's task in two ways. In the first section I tried to spell out the *nature* of teaching and teaching activities so that as intending teachers you can assess the appropriateness of your own classroom practice as well as the adequacy of approaches which may be recommended to you. The analysis is intended to help you decide what teaching really consists in so that you can evaluate your own attempts as more or less appropriate or effective.

In the second section I tried to look at various claims relating to the *scope* of the teacher's task. Here I considered the kinds of grounds on which it is sometimes argued that teachers should extend the range of their activities. I also considered current proposals which would result in a delegation of some of the teacher's traditional responsibilities to other agencies. Here the intention was to focus your attention on the implication of the teacher's involvement in the *education* of his pupils so that decisions about what activities it is either appropriate or inappropriate for teachers to regard as part of their task may be finally made by reference to this involvement.

Further reading

The following accounts provide a fuller discussion of the meaning of teaching, the nature of teaching activities in general and within educational institutions, and teaching and personal relationships: P. H. Hirst and R. S. Peters, *The Logic of Education*, Routledge & Kegan Paul, 1970, chapters 5, 6; R. S. Peters, *Ethics and Education*, Allen & Unwin, 1965, chapter 1; and R. F. Dearden, 'Instruction and Learning by Discovery', in R. S. Peters (ed.), *The Concept of Education*, Routledge & Kegan Paul, 1967.

An account of resource-based learning can be found in L. C. Taylor, *Resources for Learning*, Penguin, 1971. G. Goodacre, *Home and School*, NFER, 1970, provides a good general introduction to the topic of home–school links. Another useful collection of papers in this context is M. Craft *et al., Linking Home and School*, Longman, 1967. A. N. Sharrock, *Home/School Relations,* Macmillan, 1970, provides a select annotated bibliography.

Readers wishing to follow up the topic of school counsellors can consult *Counselling in Schools*, Schools' Council Working Paper No. 15, HMSO, 1967. The concept of the teacher as 'neutral chairman' is proposed in Schools Council Nuffield Humanities Project, *The Humanities Project, An Introduction*, Heinemann Educational Books, 1970.

Chapter two

Indoctrination

M.A.B.Degenhardt

As teachers we are liable to go wrong and expose ourselves to criticism in a variety of ways. What we teach may be false or valueless, and we shall be charged with misleading our pupils or wasting their time. Or we may be accused of incompetence when we fail to teach them anything at all. And very often teachers are accused of indoctrinating their pupils. When this happens we may be unsure of precisely what we are being accused, but we are in little doubt that something more serious than an ordinary teaching mistake is implied. For about the charge of 'indoctrination' there is a definite suggestion of profoundly influencing people in a manner that is somehow morally objectionable. At the same time, however, it remains obscure just what indoctrination is, and why it is wrong.

It is, surely, of practical importance for teachers to be clear about these two points. For if it is so very wrong to indoctrinate, do we not need to know precisely what is to be avoided, and why? And may not some teachers be so anxious to avoid indoctrination, without knowing precisely *what* they are to avoid, that they 'under-play' their proper role as educators?

Now we might expect to sort out easily what the word *means* by referring to a dictionary, but most dictionaries define 'indoctrination' as something akin to teaching and education. And this is odd when the word so often suggests something opposed to, or contrary to, education. The explanation is, I think, that in recent years talk of 'indoctrination' has tended to take on new connotations which many dictionaries have not yet got around to recording. It has become what philosophers sometimes call a pejorative or 'boo' word; a word typically used to express disapproval. It contrasts with 'hurrah' words like, for example, 'education', which typically commend or express approval.

Presumably words take on new meanings because people become aware of something new that they want to talk about or draw attention to. And this seems to be precisely the case with 'indoctrination', at least as it occurs in educational discussions. For in the twentieth century teachers have become particularly sensitive to the fact that while it is their job to influence children, some of the ways in which they can do this might be condemned as an imposition of viewpoint.

No doubt many factors have helped bring about this new sensitivity: it may be worth noting a few of them.

1   Recent centuries have witnessed the spread of what are sometimes called the 'liberal-democratic' values, which attach great importance to man's capacity to think things out for himself rather than merely accept the views of others.

2   At the same time we have become increasingly aware that we live in a world where a great variety of values, beliefs and viewpoints abounds. And once we reflect that *we* are teaching one particular set of ideas while teachers elsewhere are passing on something quite different, then we are likely to wonder about the justifiability of our own teaching.

This worry may be increased when we notice that in many countries the school curriculum is closely (often deliberately) linked to the ideals of the ruling government. We may personally feel very critical of foreign educational systems that foster, say, racialism or communism. But if we are honest must we not recognise that some observers may be equally critical when they note that in our schools religious views are expounded and mathematics lessons used to teach pupils about the stock exchange? Such considerations might lead us on to wonder if and how teachers should *ever* influence children's thinking on controversial matters: and when this happens we are at the heart of the debate about indoctrination.

3   Finally, we have become increasingly aware of the growth of a dubious area of applied psychology whereby propagandists and brainwashers have developed variously successful techniques for deliberately reshaping the thought of others. It is interesting to note that two literary works (Aldous Huxley's *Brave New World* and George Orwell's *Nineteen Eighty-Four*) first focused widespread public attention on these practices, which have since been labelled 'brainwashing'. Of course, it is absurd to suggest that a teacher in a classroom could do anything as complicated as 'brainwashing' — but could it be that in a less radical manner we wield a similarly objectionable influence over the minds of our pupils?

This, then, is the sort of background against which teachers have become sensitive to charges of indoctrination, and educational philosophers have sought to work out a clear definition of just what 'indoctrination' means. But it is difficult to achieve a generally acceptable definition, for not only is the word emotionally charged but it is used in various and sometimes inconsistent ways. Perhaps the best that can be hoped for is a definition that *approximately* corresponds to the ways in which the word has now come to be used and which may also help us to see why and how indoctrination is to be avoided.

Let us then start by examining some definitions of indoctrination that have been proposed. These have mainly consisted of attempts to show that certain types of criteria are distinctive of indoctrination. We could put the question they ask as follows: If I observe a particular activity of passing on knowledge and beliefs, and then ask whether or not this is indeed a case of indoctrination, what distinguishing features would I have to look at to settle the issue? Would it be, say, certain methods of passing on, or the content of what is taught?

Methods

At first sight it may seem that the whole question is one of methods — and that to accuse a teacher of indoctrination is to express disapproval of *how* he teaches. Suppose I spend a lesson expounding to a class my own particular views on the morality of gambling, without allowing pupils to question and discuss these — and supposing that for the next lesson I summarise these into a rhyme which the pupils then have to recite and learn by heart, would it not seem very reasonable to express disapproval of these techniques by accusing me of indoctrination?

But suppose that instead, in a classroom discussion of gambling, I try to adopt the role of neutral teacher-chairman and without actually guiding their thought, to encourage pupils to put forward, discuss and develop a variety of viewpoints of their own. Is it not hard to imagine why anybody might say *this* was indoctrination?

These and similar examples we might think of may suggest that by indoctrination we mean any one of various possible teaching methods, such as instruction without questioning, recitation and rote memorisation. Against this, however, there seem to be at least two reasons for doubting whether we can satisfactorily define indoctrination thus in terms of methods:

First, if we tried to draw up a more specific list of the offending methods, some of the items we would include might be questioned; and we would then have a debate as to whether and why 'method x' was indeed a case of indoctrination. Now does not this suggest that lying behind our discussion there must be some more general criterion in terms of which particular teaching methods might be classified as indoctrinatory or non-indoctrinatory?

Second, it seems to be the case that sometimes very similar methods of passing on ideas might or might not be regarded as indoctrination. An unquestioning recitation of the thoughts of Chairman Mao or of the Wolf-Cub's Oath might seem fairly obvious cases of indoctrination. On the other hand, if a teacher makes his pupils spend a lesson reciting difficult spellings, we might call his teaching dull or inefficient: but we would hardly say he was indoctrinating.

In general we would, I think, be inclined to regard particular methods as indoctrinatory only if they are being used to pass on controversial ideas; which is why some theorists consider that it is the content of what is passed on that matters.

Content

The argument for this criterion can take several forms: I shall try to summarise its general features before discussing whether we should accept it. It goes roughly as follows:

In some areas of thought mankind is able to establish well-founded bodies of objective knowledge such as mathematics and the natural sciences. Of course, not all scientific and mathematical viewpoints can claim to objective truth, for living and developing areas of enquiry are bound to involve disagreement and error. But, the argument runs, we do have in these areas ways of testing the truth of different theories. In science we conduct experiments and observe nature; in mathematics we use demonstration. Hence, behind their disagreements, scientists and mathematicians *are* ultimately agreed on what will settle them — what piece of evidence, for example, will help support or refute a controversial theory.

But, this argument continues, things are very different in other areas of thought about which we usually teach children. Not only are there abundant debates about politics and the arts, but these debates seem to go on and on with no prospect of ever being resolved. This, it is suggested, is because while such areas of interest have generated many viewpoints and theories, they have never established ways of testing the truth or falsity of such theories. Whereas good scientists can and do conduct experiments to test their rival theories, it is hard to see how we *can* test rival moral theories. An hour spent killing people won't tell us anything about whether murder is wrong. (Of course, there are plenty of testable propositions giving information about what people do and believe in matters of politics, religion, morality or art; but our concern here is with political, religious, moral or aesthetic propositions as such.)

The argument now concludes that to pass on information in the 'knowledge areas' (mathematics, science, etc.) is to educate, whereas to pass on positive views or 'teachings' in the belief areas we have noted is to indoctrinate.

This conclusion draws some support from the etymological connection between 'indoctrination' and 'doctrine', for we tend to think of 'doctrines' as ideas belonging to these highly controversial areas of belief. Nevertheless there are significant objections to the argument as a whole:

1   Most importantly, as is explained in chapter 6, many philosophers have good grounds for holding that the forms of knowledge are by no means as limited in number as is here suggested. Certainly the contrast between areas of knowledge and areas of belief seems to have been over-simplified. For, on the one hand, when we go deeply into subjects such as science and mathematics we find that ways of distinguishing between truth and falsity become increasingly obscure and elusive. (Indeed, the eminent contemporary philosopher of science, Sir Karl Popper, holds that we can never finally prove that a scientific law is always true: all we can do is show that some laws are false.) And on the other hand it is surely not the case that, say, moral opinions are as open and arbitrary as has been suggested. It is true, of course, that we frequently come across clashes of moral viewpoint that we seem to be unable to resolve. But it is important to note that when people disagree they do know what they are disagreeing about — which does suggest that rather elusively behind our moral disagreements lies an important area of agreement, without which moral debates would not even mean anything, and in terms of which, perhaps, moral truth and falsity are distinguishable. A similar point might be made about the other controversial areas mentioned.

2   Less conclusive in terms of the logic of the argument, but very important for the teacher, are the possibly unfortunate practical consequences of the 'content' view. For on this view the teaching of established scientific and mathematical theories would count as education, and be approved, whereas the positive teaching of moral, religious and political ideas would count as indoctrination and so be disapproved. But this is to limit severely the teacher's positive role in these tricky but important areas. Such a view will not be well received by a teacher who, surely with reason, thinks he owes it to children to give them some positive teaching and guidance on the basis of which they will, *in time,* be able to form their own autonomous judgments. Perhaps, then, a third suggested criterion, that of aims or intentions, will be more helpful.

Aims or intentions

The proposal here is that to indoctrinate is to do anything with the intention of getting people to hold views in a fixed, unquestioning way. These views may be true or false; what matters is the teacher's aim to get them accepted, and to get them accepted 'for good and all'.

This definition does seem to fit much current usage. Of two teachers presenting a particular viewpoint to their pupils, would we not label 'indoctrinator' he who was at most pains to prevent his pupils even considering the possibility of other viewpoints?

Further, such a definition effectively pinpoints what it is about indoctrination that earns our censure – for here the indoctrinator is defined as one who shows no regard for the subject's potential 'rational autonomy'.

We have already noted the great value we are inclined to attach to the human capacity for thinking things out, and reaching independent conclusions, and one who seeks to implant fixed beliefs in another is seeking to deprive him of this capacity – he is taking it upon himself to exercise for someone else that choice and judgment which, we might say, everyone has the right to exercise for himself. He is blocking the growth of those capacities, the development of which ought to be an educator's main concern.

Of course, some people may not attach great value to this capacity to develop rational autonomy; but presumably such persons will not be particularly opposed to activities of indoctrination, either.

However, one implication of the intention criterion is that by definition there can be no such thing as unintentional indoctrination. And this links to some considerations that might make us reluctant to accept this criterion as definitive.

First, it would severely limit the value of our analysis. A teacher who is anxious *not* to indoctrinate wants a definition that will tell him what not to do. To refer to his intentions is little help, for if these were not right he would hardly have raised the problem.

Second, might not a teacher be so profoundly committed to one point of view that he just cannot help presenting it in a highly persuasive manner? He is at pains to show the contrary viewpoint fairly, but inevitably he slants it according to his own outlook. And would we not say that though it is the last thing he intends, this teacher is very likely to end up indoctrinating his pupils?

A third point might be of great practical importance. In our educational thinking, are we well advised to focus all our attention on those cases where somebody deliberately sets out to influence another's thinking in a specific and restricting way? Should we not be equally attentive to less explicit and unintended ways in which the beliefs and thoughts of children are influenced? Some examples may show the sort of thing I have in mind, but that the 'intention' criteria might lead us to neglect:

Example (a)

As Plato was well aware, stories told to young children may profoundly affect the later development of their views and attitudes. Now, many of the books from which primary school children are taught to read embody a particular picture of human relations; for example, class attitudes or sex roles may be presented in a certain way.

Now, I doubt if many teachers are concerned to pass on the view that it is in the very nature of things that daddies go to work in suits, with brief-cases and umbrellas, while mummies stay at home to clean the house and cook dinner. But some children's school books do suggest just this. And is it not reasonable to suspect, just because they are unintentional and so largely unnoticed, that such influences are likely to become deeply embedded in children's minds? If somebody *tells* me something, I do at least know what I am being told; but I can pick up unreflective assumptions without myself reflecting on them.

Example (b)

A similar point can be made about the administration of an educational system: this administration may embody all sorts of notions about the people to be educated (e.g. that children categorised on the basis of exam performance should be thought of and educated in very different ways; or that different kinds of curriculum, and therefore different life-styles, are appropriate to children of different social origins). Now such assumptions *may* be unpalatable to teachers and administrators operating the system; but nevertheless they are there, shaping the way children are educated — and so, no doubt, the way they are brought to think about themselves. And again, is it not likely that the views of themselves which pupils acquire without them being made explicit are the views they will find it most difficult to reflect on and evaluate, and possibly reject?

Now it is, perhaps, hard to see how this kind of effect can be entirely avoided — for even if we took great pains to ensure that the inexplicit assumptions I have been talking about are the 'right' assumptions, this would not alter the unreflective and therefore uncritical manner in which they get picked up. But it is important to stress for the moment that to concern ourselves with indoctrination without attending to these cases at all would seem to be to altogether miss an important point.

Results

These considerations lead us finally to consider a fourth possible criterion of 'indoctrination' which makes results or effects definitive. On this account someone is said to be indoctrinated if, and in so far as, he has been brought to hold views in a fixed, unquestioning way, such that they cannot be shaken by reasons or evidence. This would enable us to say meaningfully that someone intended to indoctrinate but failed, and (what I have just suggested is very important) attend to the fact that indoctrination may have taken place without anyone having intended it to happen. Indeed, this definition seems not only to cover the important points that have already been raised, but also to direct attention on to what surely matters most: that is, on to the lasting effects on the pupil.

Does it not also correspond to the way we typically talk about indoctrination? For if we encounter someone who holds views, and either refuses or is unable to give a reasonable hearing to any objection to these views, would we not find it obviously appropriate to say he had been indoctrinated?

Moreover, to define 'indoctrination' thus in terms of fixation of belief does give (as I shall illustrate later) practical guidance to the teacher. For though, of course, we can never know for certain what will be the result of a particular piece of teaching, we can, if we know the kind of results to be avoided, begin working out how we are most likely to do this — drawing here not only on philosophical analysis, but upon psychological research and our own experience.

Despite these considerations, however, it doesn't seem *quite* right to settle for defining indoctrination exclusively in terms of the way in which someone ends up holding a particular belief. Would it not seem a bit odd to talk of indoctrination where someone holds rigidly fixed beliefs, not because of anything that has been done to him, but because he is too stupid or too idle to think things out for himself? Accordingly, I think we must qualify our position by saying that indoctrination does have to be the result of human agency or action, but it need not be a deliberate or intended result.

And we must, I think, add one further qualification, applying a kind of distinction first made by Gilbert Ryle (1949), and since used by some contemporary educational philosophers. Ryle notes that many verbs have both a 'task' and an 'achievement' sense. To take a trivial example, I might, after spending an hour sticking patches on my bicycle inner tube, say that I have been mending a puncture. And if the puncture is now repaired, I have indeed been mending it in an achievement sense; but if it turns out to be still there because I put the patches on the wrong spots, I can only be said to have been mending a puncture in the 'task' sense of 'to mend'.

Applying this distinction to our present discussion I can now, I think, propose an unavoidably cumbersome, but otherwise satisfactory definition according to which (a) indoctrination in the central and 'achievement' sense has taken place if (intentionally or unintentionally) people act on other people in a way that results in them holding fixed, unquestioning beliefs; and (b) someone is engaged in indoctrinating in a secondary and 'task' sense if he is trying, successfully or unsuccessfully, to implant fixed, unquestioning beliefs. In this way we allow for the possibilities of both intentional and unintentional indoctrination while insisting that it is something done to someone by another or others.

If this is right then it would seem that one mark of an educated man is that he holds his beliefs rationally — that is, he tends to hold beliefs only if, and in so far as, they seem to have good supporting reasons and evidence. The mark of an indoctrinated man would be that he clings to his beliefs quite irrationally, and regardless of any contrary reasons or evidence.

But a critic of the view I have suggested might find all this highly suspicious, and suggest that what I have just called education is a disguised plan for indoctrinating people with rationality. This may be a strong point against me; but I think there is a valid answer, as follows: to talk of being indoctrinated with rationality is really a contradiction in terms, since the 'job' of the word 'indoctrinate' is precisely to pick out and draw attention to ways of passing on beliefs that show no respect for the learner's rationality. It is, I think, a fairly widespread error to think of rationality as just one kind of possible viewpoint among others; but this is a mistake. I have tried to show that rationality is a matter of how we hold our beliefs. The rational man cares not just about his viewpoint, but about whether it is right, and on what grounds.

Of course, for someone to value rationality does not mean, as is sometimes suggested, that it is the only thing he values, or that he thinks everyone should strive to become completely rational and emotionless. It is doubtful whether such a human being is possible, let alone desirable. And if somebody asks us 'why be rational at all?', it is worth puzzling about what *sort* of answer I could give him: for the 'why' here is surely a request for reasons — but reasons will only be interesting to a man who is already prepared to be rational.

Furthermore a person who does believe that rationality is of no value puts himself in a very odd position indeed — for he seems to be denying the value of the capacity to think for himself without which he could not have developed this viewpoint.

So far we have had a strictly theoretical discussion of what we mean by indoctrination and why we may find it wrong. Now it is surely up to every teacher to work out for himself not only how far he accepts any argument in educational theory, but also precisely how it might guide him in the practical teaching situation, depending on such factors as what he is teaching and to whom. Accordingly, this final section will no more than briefly indicate a few of the ways in which this discussion might relate to practice.

First, then, some examples of ways in which teachers might minimise the risk of indoctrination:

1 Rousseau was surely right to advocate discovery methods in education precisely in the hope that such methods would encourage pupils to place a cautious reliance on their own judgment rather than placidly accept authority.

2 I doubt if there is any value at all in urging on children the importance of rational criticism, or of explaining what this means. But we can develop curricula that are likely to nurture such capacities. Here the practice of classroom debate and discussion is surely important: and perhaps the teacher should be concerned less with the impossible attempt at neutrality, and more with the positive initiation of discussion and provocation of thought by telling pupils of controversies of which they are ignorant, and by imaginatively and sympathetically presenting to them viewpoints which they may at first dismiss as bizarre or foolish.

3 Another way to help children to develop rationality is, of course, for their teachers to exemplify it. In particular, it would seem to be important to give reasons for the propositions and instructions we give to children: for if they are helped to see that the rightness of a particular view or action is dependent on the reasons given for it, then they are on the way to recognising that when the reasons are challenged so, too, are the conclusions.

4 It is also worth noting that certain school subjects promise to be particularly helpful as 'protectors' from indoctrination. In learning science we are, or should be, taught to consult the evidence of experience, and not to rely on authority. History and literature can not only tell us about, but help us to be sympathetic towards, modes of thought very different from those prevailing in our own culture.

Now proposals such as these might be disquieting to teachers concerned with the education of very young children. For are there not matters (the 'kerb-drill', for example) on which it is so important to get children accepting and acting on the right beliefs that only a fool will busy himself encouraging a rational-critical appraisal of the grounds for such beliefs? And do not common sense and child-psychology agree in suggesting that to fill the mind of the young child with doubts about everything would be to invite dangerous mental confusion and emotional instability?

But here, perhaps, we see another advantage of defining indoctrination in terms of effects — especially if they are long-term effects. For while it is likely that children *must* start by having a limited and largely unquestioning view of things, there is nothing to worry about so long as they do not stop at this stage. What *is* important, though, is that we try to teach children so as slowly to help them towards independent and autonomous thinking.

In this respect, however, some educators make what is surely a very serious mistake: they suggest that because of the difficulty young children are bound to find in handling controversial matters, certain subjects should not be touched on at all until they are raised in a neutral manner later on in the educational process. You may well, for example, have met the suggestion that children should have no religious education until they are, say, fifteen years old: and that then they should be presented with a variety of religious views from which to choose. However the obvious appeal of this solution is also very shallow; for it assumes that, suddenly presented with an area of thought that had been carefully kept unfamiliar, young people would be capable of understanding and appraising the views presented to them. But is it not inevitable that in such circumstances they would be puzzled and confused? Every teacher ought to be well aware that the business of acquiring concepts and understanding is long, slow and impossible for those who do not enjoy the right experiences informed by the right language usage. No one would dream of insulating children from all mathematical learning until the onset of adolescence, and then presenting them with rival mathematical theories to evaluate. Why, then, should we propose such a policy in more controversial areas of understanding? Should we not rather exert ourselves to work out ways of introducing children to these controversial areas which will advance their understanding without impairing their freedom and independence of thought?

Early in this chapter I mentioned the possibility that the well-intentioned teacher be so anxious to avoid indoctrination that he ends up doing considerably less teaching than he might. Perhaps now we can see just how mistaken, and indeed dangerous, is such an approach. For surely no one is less free, and no one more potentially a victim of indoctrination, than one who has learned nothing of the various modes of understanding which are available to man and which are discussed in chapter 6 of this book. Is it not the case that in so far as their teachers help them to acquire such modes of thought pupils are being freed by education from the threat of indoctrination?

M. A. B. Degenhardt

Further reading

Throughout this essay I am indebted in ways too numerous to specify to various papers on indoctrination. Many of these are contained in the collection edited by I. Snook under the title *Concepts of Indoctrination*, Routledge & Kegan Paul, 1972. Also important are the papers by R. Hare, and J. Wilson in T. H. B. Hollins (ed.), *Aims in Education: The Philosophical Approach*, Manchester University Press, 1964; and Snook's own book, *Indoctrination and Education*, Routledge & Kegan Paul, 1972.

Bibliography

RYLE, G. (1949), *The Concept of Mind*, Penguin ed., 1963.

Chapter three

Nature of man

D.I.Lloyd

It is said that young people in contemporary society are seeking to be
themselves, to be individuals in a society where, like plastic flowers,
they are mass-produced so that any individuality they might have is
suppressed. The existence of protest movements like the anti-Vietnam,
anti-pollution groups; the attempts to wear something which is un-
fashionable; the engagement in practices which are anti-scientific, like
the occult, all point to one thing, that the voices of individuals are
seeking to be heard in the technological, competitive and depersonalis-
ing society of today. There is a good deal of truth in this point of view
even if it is somewhat oversimplified, for there is rarely a single cause
that brings about such a widespread condition. What is undoubtedly
true is that if people are seen in a particular way, like plastic flowers, or
more familiarly, numbers, or units of production, they will be treated
as such. Or, if people are treated in a particular way, they will tend to
become seen in that way. It is, therefore, no luxury to stop and consider what our conception of man is, to see what is his nature. As
teachers, such a necessity has a double force in that we are involved in
the process which enables children to become adults, so that if our
conception of man is mistaken, our influence on children will be harmful.

In philosophy, one way of looking closely at an idea or concept is to
compare and contrast it with others. In this chapter this will be done by
contrasting the idea of 'man' with those of 'machine', 'plant' and
'animal', for at various times man has been likened to these three
things. It will be claimed that man is different in kind from these
models though the extent of his difference is less in one than in the
others. It is in the discussion of man and animal (third model) that the
fundamental difference' emerges though this is true of the other two
models also. Let us turn now to the first model.

31

D. I. Lloyd

Man as a machine

When we think of complicated machines these days we think of computers. Few can remain unimpressed by their performance. It is claimed that they can play better chess than we can, reach conclusions more quickly and write poetry with greater facility. Calculations that previously took weeks to work out now take minutes. They can store vast quantities of information and use it in any of these calculations; so that the idea that man is no more than a complex machine seems quite plausible.

This idea, that man is basically an intricate machine, is not recent; it has been around for some 300 years at least. Man has been seen as consisting of a series of levers, cogs and shafts meshing and moving according to some predetermined end. Thomas Hobbes, an English philosopher, saw the whole of man in mechanical terms. Later, the French writer La Mettrie called one of his works *L'Homme machine.* He wrote: 'Let us consider boldly that man is a machine and that in the whole universe there is but a single substance variously modified.' He believed that human beings were nothing but matter, and thinking and feeling its movements. They are subject to physical laws, so that the study of human nature becomes a branch of physics. If we hold such a mechanistic view, does this mean that we have to give up the idea that there is a mind somewhere inside our body? In general the answer is yes, though some have been less radical by arguing that mind does exist but is a by-product of matter and is still subject to those same physical laws.

This mechanistic view is no longer held in this form, but there are quite reputable views today which belong to the same tradition. Chemistry and biochemistry, in particular, are subjects which have led some thinkers to believe that what happens to us and what we do can be explained by physical laws. The functions of the body such as respiration and digestion are seen to be purely chemical and are not imbued with some special 'living' force. The discovery of DNA has shown that the passing on of hereditary characteristics and the process of growth are really no more than particular chemical processes. In the end everything, it is claimed, is basically matter and we are all variations on a chemical theme. Does this mean, we may ask, that there is nothing distinctive about man? The answer to this question is attempted in full when examining our third model. At least two things can be said here. First, the model does not help us to understand the difference between a lifeless object and a living organism as we generally know them, and so cannot help us in understanding the variety of feelings and emotions a man has. Second, if we were to regard children as mere machines (or chemical substances), we would no longer have respect for them as people in their own right, but would repair them if they went wrong, or dispose of them if they were beyond repair. Yet we do have a moral relationship with other people, and if this is left out of our account of man we omit something very important.

Clearly, many people have not taken a position of the kind outlined above. They may not have a well thought out mechanistic view of human nature. Yet the language of mechanics may nevertheless influence our attitude towards others in a much more subtle way. Even in education the idea of its institutions being pieces of mechanism is not entirely a thing of the days when Andrew Bell planned his monitorial school as he would a steam engine. Today colleges and schools are sometimes spoken of as factory plant with a measurable output and wastage. Of course no one would say that they were treating people and places as machines and factories, but the borrowing of language from the field of mechanics makes the move from metaphor to literalness much easier.

Of this model then we can say that we are helped by it in so far as it helps us to understand that our movements are not totally random and arbitrary, that there are laws and principles which lie behind what we think; that there is planning, order and progress. The inadequacy of the model lies in the amount of human behaviour which is left out if the model is taken as a complete account of the nature of man.

Man as a plant

If we move to our second model, man as a plant, we detect some improvement over our previous model. Instead of the teacher being a mechanic constructing and repairing an inorganic thing, here we have a gardener nurturing an organic object. The machine does not grow whereas a plant does. This model, then, does seem to be more applicable to teaching than the last, for as Scheffler (1960, pp. 47–50) points out: 'In both cases, the developing organism goes through phases that are relatively independent of the efforts of gardener or teacher. In both cases, however, the development may be helped or hindered by these efforts.' And later: 'In neither case is the gardener or the teacher indispensable to the development of the organism and, after they leave, the organism continues to mature.' Both gardener and teacher are keen to ensure the right conditions are provided. It is no wonder that quite a large number of people in education, usually known as progressives, regard the idea of growth as central to their beliefs. What the idea does is to redefine the teacher–pupil relationship from an authoritarian one to a more modest one. It embodies the idea of helping rather than constructing, nurturing rather than building, and the recognition that such an organism will go through different stages, some more critical for its existence than others. As a consequence a good deal of knowledge of children on the one hand and flexibility in attitude on the other is demanded of teachers.

When that is all said we still have to ask the following crucial question. How are we to recognise whether a child is growing up in the embryonic way that, say, is comparable to the way in which a tulip grows? We know tulips will become tulips and nothing more, but what of children? Here we come to the limitations of the analogy. Whilst a child is born with physical and temperamental characteristics, all manner of interests, attitudes, ambitions and values are consistent with the *same* physical growth. The social environment for the child has a much more important effect than the physical environment for the plant. There is a dimension of life which is absent in the world of botany. This a baby does not bring with him into the world, but is something he acquires in his contact with adults and other children. For example, a child may acquire an interest in bird-watching, be able to repair simple machines, have some liking for music, be an ardent churchgoer, or have regard for the aged. Such acquisitions are by no means built into his nature at birth, but are the result of various influences that surround him. If he were elsewhere, it is not hard to imagine that he would have developed quite differently. When we speak, then, in education of helping a child to 'realise himself', 'to become what he wants', we underplay the role environment plays in enabling him to have such possibilities in the first place. This is what is meant by saying that all manner of ways and styles of life are consistent with the same physical development. R. F. Dearden (1968, ch. 3) discusses this whole question and examines the mistake of assuming that one can say what a child should grow into from understanding his physical environment alone. It is to make the error which is known in philosophy as deriving an 'ought' from an 'is', i.e. deriving judgments of value from matters of fact. Dearden says (p. 34) that 'no growth theorist is going to admit that Hitler "grew", in the lauded, ideological sense of "grew" '. This shows that we only use the idea of growth and development rather than stunting and distortion when we agree with what a child is doing.

The value of the growth model is high. It helps us to see that the child is a developing organism having different features at different points during the period of development. For the teacher this means the relationship with his pupil is much more complex and delicate and demands a greater sensitivity on his part than if he adopted a mechanical view.

The limitation of the idea is that it goes too far in ascribing a finished form to the child and prevents us from seeing that a variety of habits, attitudes, interests and values are all at home with the notion of growth. We now turn to the last model, man as an animal.

Man as an animal

Here we seem to be much nearer the nature of man. In fact, whereas man is never talked of as being a plant but rather like one, he is regarded as being an animal. One ability which animals possess which plants do not, is the ability to learn. They can learn anything from how to find food to how to perform circus tricks. Their physiological make-up is more complex than that of a plant. Pigeons learn how to discriminate between shades of colours, rats find their way through mazes, dogs wheel prams in circuses and chimpanzees co-operate with tea firms to make TV advertisements. In recent years psychologists have studied the behaviour of animals and the abilities that they can acquire. It has been felt that they can throw a good deal of light on the way that human beings learn. In zoology the cries of birds, the dances of bees, the instincts of seals have been the subjects of observation. Then, too, we know more than ever before of the complicated but fascinating habits of all kinds of animals. Such knowledge may lead us to think that there is no real difference in kind between animals and men, and, in fact, that animals are in some respects more developed than we are. Darwin was one who thought that there was a natural continuity between man and animal. Some of his admirers disagreed with him on this point. Lloyd Morgan, a famous psychologist and an admirer of Darwin, believed that there was an essential difference between the two kinds in that it was only man who possessed 'consciousness'. He believed, as have many at all times, that man has more than the capacity for seeing and hearing; he also has the unique capacity for self-consciousness which enables him to think and learn about himself. Man is on a higher plane altogether. In reply someone might object by saying that animals can think and learn just as man can. This is true, but this way of putting it glosses over the differences between them in the kind of things they are capable of learning. Whilst dogs can learn their owners' movements, and seals can balance balls better than humans, neither seems to be able to talk. Even if one grants that they can communicate, again it would be misleading to leave the matter there. The calls and sounds of animal life do alter the behaviour of other animals, yet the difference lies in what they can communicate, and what kind of behaviour is being altered. Take the various forms that talking can take — chatting, gossiping, ordering, questioning, grumbling, praising and so on. These distinctions within human communication are possible because of what man has to communicate, his ideas, his knowledge. He has behind him a long tradition of experience and ideas about birth, marriage, death, work, leisure, and within those aspects of human life there are, as we know, vast variations. We speak of the life a man leads, whereas we speak of the life of the bee. A man's life is the result of a large number of decisions that have been made by him and for him. Such decisions involve understanding other people and their desires. They involve, more basically, symbols of communication and seeing the world in a particular way. This is the central difference being claimed here between man and the other three models. This idea of understanding is peculiar to man and any attempt to treat him in such a way that this is diminished needs to be justified. In the remainder of the chapter, this particular point will be illustrated by three examples. Each of them is sufficient on its own to make the point in general, but three such examples have the value of showing the main thesis from different vantage points.

Example (a)

Some years ago, I read an amusing description of what an African anthropologist might see if he visited the Brighton beach in the middle of summer. I cannot remember the source or exact words used but it read something like this.

The people of England are religious and devout worshippers of the sun. Each year they leave their homes and travel to the coast for the purpose of worship and often take up small accommodation in tents or in what they call caravans, or live with other people during their short stay. Each day they begin worship by prostrating themselves on the shingle in the heat of the sun, which is often so hot that they wear shields over their eyes. Their bodies become burnt and some become ill, but few are deterred by this, such is their devotion. At various times people will baptise themselves in the waters, calling to each other and waving their arms in ecstasy. At midday, families group together when a symbolic ceremony takes place. Three-cornered pieces of bread, known to the natives as 'sandwiches', are passed around and eaten. During the afternoon they throw symbolic, large, inflated, multi-coloured orbs to one another, illustrating the dominance of the sun in their lives. Throughout all this, the elders lie motionless in their canvas seats with their faces covered, in deep and prolonged meditation. These observances may continue for a family for up to fourteen days, when they return to their work until the following year.

The general point here may be put like this. The above interpretation of what the people on Brighton beach were doing is quite consistent with their physical movements. That is to say, that if these people really were sun-worshipping instead of sunbathing and enjoying themselves, their bodily movements would be no different. The difference lies in how they saw their movements. What the anthropologist did not do was to see things the way the natives did, to entertain the ideas they had and to understand the significance that these things had for them. So it is the *understanding,* which is non-physical and cannot be handled, which makes this difference. This is shown by the fact that it was possible for a physical movement to be interpreted in different ways. In this example the point that emerges is two-edged, for it also means that if we *are* to understand what a person is doing we must understand his ideas. An over-enthusiastic psychologist might interpret a child's hitting another on the back as an act of aggression. On the contrary, in some areas it would be a sign of affection. A wink across the classroom may mean 'Hello', 'You're my best friend', 'I'll get you playtime' or 'We've got the teacher where we want him'. One may show that interpreting a particular bodily movement in one way may show ignorance of the way that that action is seen by the person performing it, as was so in the anthropologist's case. Language occurs in the social context and its meaning is particular to that context. It seems to me that teachers of children both of different social backgrounds and different races from their own need to take the trouble to learn the significance of the language and behaviour of such children from the children themselves if they are to teach them anything. Otherwise they will, as often happens, pass each other by. In our second example, unlike the first example where the wrong action was attributed, the mistake of the observer lies in attributing a human action where there is none.

Example (b)

Mary is ten years old. Her sister, Janet, is two years old. They go shopping together. In one shop Mary takes a game and Janet a bar of chocolate, both without paying. They arrive home, are questioned and it is found out that they have taken them from the shop. They are both given a hiding.

Let us ignore the form of punishment meted out and concentrate on the fact that both were regarded as guilty, not just of taking something without paying, but of stealing. It could be rightly said of Mary that she should have known better. She knew what she was doing. But of Janet we would have said the opposite. She did not know what she was doing. The difference between them is that only one of them understood ideas such as buying and selling, payment and ownership. We can, then, only describe an action as stealing because we withhold the description of stealing from an action performed by someone who does not have these ideas. As in the first example, the physical movements of both sisters are identical; we only attribute a wrong action to Mary because she had an idea and a grasp of what she was doing, and that literally makes a world of difference. This in turn leads us to withhold blame from the younger child. We do not hold her responsible for what, under different conditions — namely, where she *could* understand like her sister — would be stealing. In teaching, if all we were trying to do was to get children to move their limbs in particular ways, we could never make the kind of distinction just made.

In teaching we not only enable children to grasp ways of communicating but also, as a recent philosopher puts it, 'give them something to communicate.' Subjects on the school curriculum are intended to achieve precisely this. They are intended to open up new forms of understanding, new kinds of behaviour. This all sounds rather grand but a look at any school subject will demonstrate this in a particular way (see chapter 6).

In the third example, we have the reverse of the second example. In this case, instead of attributing an action to someone who did not merit it, as in Janet's case, we have an illustration of denying the attribution of a human action to someone who does deserve it.

Example (c)

Professor Eysenck, in a recent television broadcast, was discussing the question whether 'conscience is a conditioned reflex'. He wanted to say it was. He would describe Mary's action as just the result of a conditioned reflex, and would reject the contention that what she did was morally wrong. Here, in my terms, he is translating what I have earlier regarded as a feature of human life into one of animals, namely conditioned reflexes. To support his view he quotes a famous experiment by R. L. Solomon where six-month-old puppies were given the choice of two kinds of meat, horsemeat and a commercially produced dog food. When the puppies chose the horsemeat they were struck with rolled-up newspaper. In this way they became conditioned to avoiding the horsemeat. The succeeding two days they were given no food, but after that time were given a dish of horsemeat. Eysenck comments that those who did take some horsemeat showed certain emotional reactions, which he calls 'guilt reactions'. What Eysenck obtains, he believes, from this experiment is support for his claim that 'conscience is simply a conditioned reflex', and the more general claim that human morality is the result of social conditioning. That is, every belief we have and every action we perform is not the result of moral reasoning but of our being made to feel guilty. The point Eysenck misses is that in order to feel guilty you must be able to recognise something as moral. He makes it sound as if the animals *see* the taking of horsemeat as immoral. R. Beardsmore in his *Moral Reasoning* (p. 52) points out that he cannot have it both ways. He cannot say guilt is no more than being conditioned and then also say that they see what they are doing as being morally wrong. In fact, why should he want to use the word 'guilt' here at all in relation to the puppies? Why not just 'fear'? He presumably has an idea of what moral is before he goes on to say that it is not really moral. The attempt to translate human behaviour into animal behaviour fails. It is like trying to argue that a church, school or museum is no more than a collection of bricks (but one must have already the idea of a school before saying that). Of course these buildings are made of bricks but that does not mean that they are *merely* bricks. In the same way it is true that a man is an animal, but that is not to say he is no more than an animal. To put it another way, it is as misleading to say all moral behaviour is the result of conditioning as it is to say all buildings are no more than putting one brick on top of another. Certainly moral behaviour is the result of learning, but *what* a child learns is different from what an animal learns. Even if one accepts Eysenck's view that morality is a matter of conditioning, what he ignores is that the behaviour and reactions that human beings can be conditioned into displaying is quite different in kind from that of animals. We may wish to speak of the Germans in the 1930s as being conditioned to accept anything that Hitler said as being infallible, or of the Western World today as being conditioned into thinking that the value of life is determined by your most recent possessions. Even if you are prepared to call that conditioning, I have never heard of anyone claiming that animals can be conditioned into having those kinds of beliefs.

Professor Eysenck seems to be guilty, if I may use the word, first of reducing or translating moral behaviour (which we normally contrast with conditioning) into conditioning and, more to our point, of implying that conditioning is of only one kind, the kind to which animals are susceptible. In this way he is glossing over the differences between humans and what they can learn. Dr Drury, in chapter 2 of *The Danger of Words,* in criticising Eysenck, points out that his language has become increasingly physiological of late, which in turn implies that he is getting further away from the human world of understanding. Eysenck seems to be assuming that a further knowledge of brain processes connected with conditioning is of help in understanding the nature of man. But knowledge of the chemical constituents of bricks and the principles of building construction do not help us one bit in understanding the difference between a church and a prison. Of course, we cannot think, have such ideas, or engage in a human way of life without a body, or think without a brain; but having a brain does not, of itself, produce those ideas. Nevertheless, it is not uncommon these days to find people attempting to discuss human features in animal terms.

In all three examples, what has been attempted is to show that the essential feature of man is his possession of understanding. This places him apart and on a different plane from anything else. The nature of his life takes on a new form and a different character. Of course, this aspect of his life is only one of many. His understanding of nature and his appreciation of beauty could serve to show this difference. The point of using moral understanding is that unlike science and art, morality must always enter our lives. This must apply to teaching. There is no occasion when we are not in a moral relationship with our pupils, though science and art may be taught for only a short period in a week. A mistaken conception of man concerning his moral understanding may therefore lead, as was pointed out earlier, not only to a confusion about what we are going to teach but how we are going to teach. That we are teaching children makes a considerable difference. If they were not human we might consider doing other things which might make life simpler but at the expense of all that we consider right.

I know of no more dramatic and telling way to make this point than to end with a reference to Swift's ironical comment on British management of Irish affairs in the eighteenth century. In a short article entitled 'A Modest Proposal . . .' he tells us that there are tens of thousands of unwanted babies in Ireland. There are far too many to be cared for and provided for. The obvious solution, says Swift, is for us to sell and eat them, and he suggests some dishes. In a cool and efficient way he lists the advantages that such proposed new kind of stock-raising would have for the country. His argument is faultless, except for one thing – the children happen to be human.

Further reading

As the most common way in which man is regarded is as an animal, a more detailed reading of Professor E. J. Eysenck's description of and comment on the Solomon experiment in his book *Fact and Fiction in Psychology,* Penguin, 1965, repays study. R. W. Beardsmore's helpful remarks on this are in *Moral Reasoning,* Routledge & Kegan Paul, 1969, pp. 51–3. R. Rhees's article 'Learning and Understanding' in his collection *Without Answers,* Routledge & Kegan Paul, 1969, ch. 15, and Dr M. O'C. Drury's ch. 2 of *The Danger of Words,* Routledge & Kegan Paul, 1973, are refreshingly non-technical but provide helpful insight into this matter.

Bibliography

DEARDEN, R. F. (1968), *Philosophy of Primary Education,* Routledge & Kegan Paul.
HOBBES, THOMAS (1968 ed.), *Leviathan,* Penguin.
LA METTRIE, J. DE (1747), *L'Homme machine,* quoted in Isodor Chein, *The Science of Behaviour and the Image of Man,* Tavistock, 1972.
MORGAN, C. LLOYD (1896), *Habit and Instinct,* New York.
SCHEFFLER, I. (1960), *The Language of Education,* Blackwell.
SWIFT, J. (1932), 'A Modest Proposal for Preventing the Children of Ireland from being a burden to their Parents or Country', in *Satires and Personal Writings,* ed. W. A. Eddy, Oxford University Press.

Chapter four

Aims of education

P.J. Higginbotham

Teachers make decisions about what to do in school, about what to teach and how to teach it, about what to pass on and what to ignore. Their reasons for these decisions may vary and indeed any single decision may depend, not on one, but on several reasons. Yet these will normally include some kind of notion (more or less explicit) both of the aims of education generally and of a particular lesson or course. Thus an eleven-year-old class, for example, engaged in writing an English composition may be so occupied just because this is the way by which the teacher can get them settled down to work; equally it may be that this activity is planned to ensure that they will acquire the skills of literacy essential for GCE in later years, and in this case a requirement thought to be necessary by both parents and the State: yet again such learning may have been selected by the teacher as a means of involving the pupils in worthwhile experiences, and of helping them acquire worthwhile skills. These reasons, expediency, the demands of parents and society, the value implicit in the activity itself, or its result, must in some way affect the way in which the teacher goes about the task. They are in part the criteria by which the teacher selects what to do and what he hopes to achieve: further, they are the means by which the success or failure of the activity can be assessed. In this sense they are the aims or the objectives of the activity, an activity which is part of the educational process. Similarly, to talk of the aim of a mathematics course as the achievement of an A-level pass in pure mathematics is to give a specific objective to this course and one which can be evaluated.

In all these instances we imply that it is possible, prior to carrying out a task, to have a clearly outlined *objective* which is usually used as the criterion by which we evaluate how far we have succeeded in the task. It is useful to use the term 'objective' here to distinguish between the idea of an immediate aim for part of the educational process and the long term aims of education. Hence, 'objective' usually relates to an end or process which will be aimed at in the specific task or lesson. The objective may be the achievement of a skill such as reading or the mastery of a technique such as the handling of scientific experiments. It may be the development and clarification of certain concepts such as 'conservation', and 'right action', or the exploration of some aspect of creativity such as the writing of poetry. Yet, these objectives will dictate to some extent the way in which the activity is undertaken and also the content of that activity. They also suggest ways by which we evaluate the degree of success which has been achieved.

If, however, when we consider the total education experienced by an individual, or the education offered by particular schools, we ask — what is the aim of such an education? — we imply a concern with the end to which the overall experience has been directed. Thus a group of ex-pupils discussing their different school experiences may well discover that though some schools appear to agree on the end aimed at in their education, yet the routes to this end differ considerably. This same group of pupils may equally discover that in other cases schools which appear to have different ends are nevertheless offering their pupils educational experiences which are often very similar. Thus of two schools aiming to give a sound general education, one might seek to do so by means of courses covering a wide range of subjects, the other by courses in specially selected subjects. Alternatively, two schools, one aiming to provide a highly specialised academic education and one aiming at a sound general education (development of a literate and numerate population) might at some point offer their pupils very similar courses in languages, literature, mathematics and science. Schools can thus seek to achieve similar educational aims by pursuing different paths to them. Similarly schools with differing aims may yet have certain courses in common. It is clear on reflection however that at some point differences in educational aims must make a marked and significant difference to what goes on within the educational process — and this can best be seen when we consider the difference in the education systems of, say, a Western democracy and Communist China.

Aims of education

Aims of education normally refer to long-term general ends, often difficult to define clearly in terms of specific behaviour. Thus, we talk of aiming to produce the Philosopher Ruler (Plato's *Republic*), or men able to use their leisure properly (Aristotle); of aiming to bring a person to emotional and intellectual maturity or to ensure that children learn how to learn. Such general statements differ in the extent to which they make clear what we as teachers should be doing. Aristotle's emphasis on learning to use 'leisure properly' is more informative than a statement about emotional and intellectual maturity, yet even it requires a considerable examination of what is entailed in 'using leisure properly' before we can use this as a basis for planning an educational programme. Long-term aims of education must inevitably have some degree of generality but it is important to make such statements of aims throw some light on the actual task we set out to do. Long-term aims do, however, direct attention to the total educational experience of a person. They seem, in contrast to objectives, to emphasise the acquiring of attitudes, skills and insights which have to do with a person's overall capacity to function as a human being, and such a capacity, it will be argued later in the chapter, has something to do with the person's autonomy on the one hand and his membership of society on the other.

It is useful for purposes of clarity to distinguish in educational discussion between long-term aims and immediate objectives, but it also makes teachers aware that they make decisions in both areas. Further, the general aim of education which a teacher holds must logically relate in some way to his immediate objectives. The establishment of only a general aim of education would make for difficulties in trying to evaluate the achievement of particular tasks selected in the process of teaching and lay the teacher open to the risk of vagueness and lack of direction. For though a general aim does not directly dictate particular objectives, it can and perhaps ought to act as a standard against which the value of all planned activities can be judged. In this way a generalised aim gives a direction and coherence to the pupil's total educational experience. In the examples mentioned earlier of a particular English lesson or teaching A-level mathematics it must affect in some way the choice of objective and the approach to the work. It also affects the relationship of the parts of the total educational experience to one another. An *aim* of education implies a target to be reached with a certain direction of movement even though there may be a number of ways to get there. This analogy of a target can be misleading and oversimplify our understanding of how these general aims in education affect our judgment about the success of any particular school in educating its pupils; for they, in trying to decide how far their own education has achieved its aims, are in danger of assuming that they have arrived at the target when they leave school, little realising that the immediate effect of an experience is often vastly different from the long-term one. Though this may imply difficulty in evaluating the success of an education achieving its general aims, it does not affect what the writer sees as the central function of such aims — namely that they give direction and coherence to the pupil's total educational experience. The other side to this question is to ask whether we do need to have a general aim of education at all? The case against having such a general aim is argued for by Pring (1973, p. 46).

Before we can begin to consider what our educational aims ought to be, we need first to note two different notions implicit in the word education. It can refer to the actual *process* of education in which pupils participate and also to the *achievement* resulting from this process. In talking about either general aims or the objectives of a particular activity we may focus on either the process or the achievement aspect of the word. The objectives in A-level mathematics could be the achievement of an A-level pass *or* certain kinds of mathematical experience to be gained by pupils. The aims of education could be either a range of learning experiences (the process) to be offered or the acquiring of certain skills, attitudes and insights (the achievement).

Further, any attempt to sort out what our education aims ought to be requires us to consider what is implicit in the concept of education itself and also in the relationship between the demands of society and those of the individual. Since schooling and education are part of a society's function it is inevitable that the task of its schools should be seen, partly, as preparing the young for living in that society. In our society this means training people for innovation and at the same time transmitting our culture. In addition, Illich (1971, pp. 2–12) draws our attention to the school's 'hidden curriculum' in terms of a pupil's future job expectations, and how the school in this sense acts as an allocator to future occupations. In practice the demand for public examination successes, and paper qualifications, reflects this pressure from society on education. The demand for literacy and numeracy, for adaptability and the capacity to use leisure wisely, reflects society's pressure for the school to be concerned with innovation, while the demand for a relevant curriculum and for moral and political education also reflects society's concern to preserve itself.

Whilst society makes demands which inevitably affect the aims of education of its teachers, so too does the individual person make claims to which consideration must be given. Behind any notion of education lies an assumption about the nature of man as a person. In the assessment of what distinguishes him from other forms of life or from machines it is clear that language plays a significant part. Through its use, men communicate and share their feelings and ideas. It extends their awareness and understanding of other people and of situations different from their own. Through discussion we clarify experiences and come to establish a shared and, therefore, public body of knowledge. Further, because through language we come to understand situations in which we find ourselves so we are able to plan, to make rules which we can choose to follow or to reject and to have standards by which we evaluate these experiences. Thus conceptually, man can be seen as capable of following rules, of establishing standards and of giving reasons for his actions. Behaviour which shows such awareness of choice and the possibility of planned action seems to exemplify what are the distinguishing features of a human being. The development of such distinguishing characteristics in men is to be found in their

capacity to handle knowledge, to reason and to make informed judgments — R. S. Peters (1965, pp. 47—55) talks of 'the hallmark of mind'
and goes on to argue that a teacher must be concerned with what he
terms the 'consciousness of his pupils'. Any long-term aim of education
must then take into account the necessity to develop this consciousness
in human beings, and to ensure the development of an enquiring mind.
Whatever education may be, it surely ought not to involve processes
which lead to pupils responding like automatons, or passively accepting
all that is handed on without question or doubt. Though the pressures
and demands of society may require that examinations be passed, that
knowledge be learnt and skills mastered, yet there are different ways of
achieving these things, and the way in which they are achieved and the
way in which they inform the mind of the learner is all important.

The demands which society and the individual make on education
often appear to be in conflict. Current arguments in favour of a specialised rather than a general education, especially at sixth-form level, or
for a vocational rather than a liberal education, often cite society's need
for more highly specialised citizens such as scientists and technologists
as against the individual's right to achieve his full potential as a person.
Reconciling such conflicting demands is a complex problem and not
one to which a solution in general terms can be given. Yet that such
demands exist makes us look more closely at the concept of education
itself and ask, first, what characteristics mark it out as something particular and, second, whether all schooling (everything that goes on in
school or college) is in fact educational. Only then can we make decisions about the aims of education.

Education as has been explained in an earlier section of this chapter
can mean two different things, the process and the achievement, so that
we can ask on what grounds we could call a person educated, and on
what grounds we could call a process educational. People normally use
the word education to describe something they approve of, so many
people would argue that the use of the word education implies that
something valuable has been achieved, or that the process is, by implication, valuable. We would therefore exclude from what we call education
teaching people to take drugs, avoid their income tax or to steal. Similarly, we would surely exclude on moral grounds learning how to kill
others even if it were hoped that awareness of such acts might lead to a
greater respect for life. Thus for something to be educational both the
content and the actual process must be seen to be worthwhile. This
notion seems to exclude what is trivial, worthless or, even more so,
objectionable. Clearly then, what goes on in school is not necessarily
always educational, as for example collecting dinner money or wasting
time at various points in the day. The decisions as to what learning
experiences and what content are selected for the school curriculum
and how to engage pupils in work must radically affect whether what

goes on in school is mere schooling or whether it can count as education. If we accept that education carries with it the implication that it is of value, we can proceed to examine what other characteristics the word appears to imply, either in referring to the achievement or to the actual process.

Educational achievement

In talking of the educational achievement of a particular school it may seem a truism to say that the aim has been to produce an educated person, yet this does direct attention to what we envisage as the worthwhile element in education, it does make us ask the questions: what is it which makes education valuable?, and how can we recognise this in the educated man? The claim that a person who has gained five O-level passes in GCE is an educated man might well be challenged. A degree in physics or skill in practical plumbing does not in itself establish that their possessor is an educated man; for a highly skilled examinee with no love or genuine understanding of his subject and a plumber with skill but little understanding of its underlying theory would both lack the expertise and perspective necessary to make informed judgments when applying what they have learned to a variety of problems. If such learning does not enable them in the future to make sound judgments then it seems justifiable to deny that they are educated men. Thus the schooling which leads to an educated man must ensure a deepening of understanding and awareness of knowledge which will inform the learners' future action. To consider these two examples in more detail, the plumber whose understanding of what he is about and whose knowledge relevant to the job inform his practical skills could well be said to have been educated into his craft. The physicist able not only to reproduce his knowledge but to explore his field of study and to judge critically relevant research could be said to be educated into physics. Yet, even so, to claim that they are 'educated men' would appear exaggerated, for the phrase seems ideally to imply a kind of 'wholeness' in the person's experience and outlook. R. S. Peters (1965, p. 46) argues that an educated man is one who has achieved 'a cognitive perspective' which informs and affects his understanding of all aspects of his life. Thus for the plumber or physicist to be an educated man, he must have acquired an attitude of mind and breadth of knowledge which inform how he comes to see the world. The need for 'wholeness' means that there must be a minimum range of study and limits the degree of specialisation possible, so raising a question about the extent of specialisation and breadth of study necessary for the production of an educated man. Any attempt then to spell out the aim of education in terms of its achievement must recognise this cognitive element as a necessary constituent and must include the development of knowledge in such a way that it will inform a person's judgments.

Educational process

In talking of the educational process experienced in a particular school, we have to decide what makes it educational. To do so we must bear in mind the conditions in which the process takes place and we have already seen that it must involve the development of knowledge and understanding which will inform a person's outlook. Further, the content selected must be seen to be of value if it is to count as education. Hence all the different activities which go to make up the process must, if they are to count as education, satisfy certain criteria. Some would argue that the process is one of nurturing or fostering development but the writer proposes here to use what seems an interpretation more relevant to education, namely that it is a process of initiation. In discussing this idea in his inaugural lecture, 'Education as Initiation', (1963, p. 38) R. S. Peters argues that a process is not normally educational unless it satisfies criteria relating to:

(a) the content of the transaction between teacher and taught,

(b) the nature of the interpersonal element in the transaction, and

(c) the development of a cognitive perspective.

We may instruct or train, we may help pupils to make discoveries or solve problems. The question is, when are such activities educational? First, the content must be deemed to be valuable by public standards. The grounds on which it is possible to justify the inclusion of some experiences as more worthwhile than others is something that must be considered (Peters, 1965, ch. 5). To train in the skill of bayonet charging might be necessary for survival but could not in itself be regarded as valuable and as such would not be part of education. Second, the nature of the transaction, be it training, instruction or discovery, must also be examined. The master craftsman handing on his own skills and the secrets (knowledge) of his craft, both in training and in giving guidance, is surely educating his apprentices. This is because of the nature of the relationship between teacher and taught. The craftsman is concerned that his apprentices understand and come to care about the skills, and seeks to initiate them into this body of practical knowledge which is regarded as valuable not just by him but by others too. He cares both about the craft he is handing on and about initiating his apprentices. Equally, his apprentices share that concern since they have chosen to enter into an apprenticeship. In contrast, it is possible for present-day apprentices, compelled to attend college on a day-release basis, to be instructed in a theory apparently far removed from practice, and expressed in technical language of a kind they are unfamiliar with and neither comprehend nor want to learn. Their practical training and the theoretical underpinning may not ever come together to inform each other. Thus, the nature of the transaction between teacher and pupils would make it difficult for such a process to be educational. This example further illustrates the significance of Peters's third criterion of an educational process in that the master craftsman, initiating apprentices to his craft, does far more than develop in his pupils certain skills and a caring for the craft. His 'informed' judgment lies at the root of his skill and gives, in Peters's words, 'a cognitive perspective' to his work, and this too is part of what he passes on to the apprentices. It may well be suggested that a master craftsman might lack a cognitive perspective because he did not articulate his understanding in symbolic form, but the writer would argue that such a craftsman could communicate his understanding to others even though the means of doing so might depend on a very minimal amount of public language and a considerable amount of non-verbal communication. His cognitive perspective would show, however, in his judgment and sensitivity to his craft and the way in which this informed his view of other aspects of life. For the teachers of today's apprentices, opportunity for the exercise of this informed judgment in relating theory and practice may well be more limited. Similarly, the good examinee trained in exam techniques may lack the insight and understanding to apply his knowledge and, though trained, lack cognitive awareness. A mathematician, on the other hand, whose awareness of his subject enables him to appreciate the elegance of a proof and who is able to let this spill over into his approach to knowledge in general, can be said to have been engaged in an educational process.

In illustrating what has been argued in this section on the idea of an educational process, the master craftsman example shows clearly how what is taught must bear the stamp of worthwhileness. Thus the teacher must be able to justify it by public standards and must seek to make the learner come to care for it too. Once the content of learning has been decided then attention must be turned to how to initiate into such learning. Peters (1965, pp. 41–5) argues that there must be a 'minimum of willingness and voluntariness' on the part of the learner, and this would certainly rule out certain morally unacceptable procedures, such as brainwashing. Some forms of pain reinforcement and compulsory training may bring about learning, but such compulsion seems to deny man's humanity. To reject such procedures does not mean that we expect all pupils to come willingly to class or be highly motivated but it does establish limits beyond which the process ceases to be educational. It means that there must be some degree of comprehension however little, and a minimal degree of freedom to choose to participate in order for the transaction to be educational. Finally, such a transaction must be aimed at increasing the learner's knowledge and understanding in such a way that they will inform his actions and judgments. Any aim of education must give due attention to our understanding of man's developing mind and it is for this reason that this emphasis on the cognitive element is so important.

The immediate objectives and long-term aims of education

The immediate objectives and long-term aims of education which teachers have must inevitably be affected by their concept of education. In deciding what to transmit and how to engage pupils in learning and developing their understanding and awareness, teachers are making judgments which reflect their idea of an educated man and an educational process. Yet these decisions are not always easy to justify. We can easily justify the decision to initiate children into reading on utilitarian grounds and by citing the demands of society. We could, less easily, justify it in terms of its intrinsic worthwhileness. But a decision to teach a whole range of traditional subjects in the curriculum rather than a topic based on the local community would require a much more complex justification and would be more open to challenge. Further, since a pupil's education goes on over a period of years and is carried out by different schools and different teachers, these are good grounds for having aims of education to give coherence and continuity to the process. Admittedly, a teacher's decision about objectives and long-term aims will depend in part on the learner's capacity for education. This means that the aims of education for infant, junior, secondary and special schools must be expressed in objectives which will be appropriate to the pupils in these different schools, yet such aims must surely ensure the achievement of this continuity and coherence. It is the aim of education held by the teacher and that expressed tacitly if not explicitly by the school community which will determine the quality of the learning experiences and give such coherence. Yet the teacher and school are subject to the pressures and demands of parents, society in general, and, today, pupils themselves: these are demands for tangible achievements and the acquiring of knowledge relevant to society. Further, society itself may, because of its multi-cultural basis, need as never before to be concerned with the development in its citizens of rational judgment and moral awareness. It is in this area that the demands of society would seem to link with those of the individual; for in discussing the nature of man earlier in this chapter it was suggested that education must be concerned with the development of an 'enquiring mind'. This implies not only the acquisition of knowledge and understanding but also training in the early years so that the questioning and enquiry in later years may be based on a sound understanding of what is involved in acting responsibly and independently. Thus the individual's demand for rational autonomy would seem to have something in common with society's demand for citizens capable of rational judgment and moral awareness.

It is important to note that the concept of education suggested here implies that education is pursued for what is valuable in it, that is for its intrinsic worth. The demand for tangible achievements, in the form of examinations and qualifications, suggests extrinsic aims which can be achieved in ways which are independent of (or at variance with) what we understand by education. The demand for rational moral agents and for rational autonomy suggests aims which could truly be educational since for men to achieve rational automony and to act morally they would need to be initiated into a range of worthwhile experiences and to acquire understanding and knowledge through the kind of teacher—pupil interaction that Peters suggests. Thus the aims of schooling may well pursue both utilitarian objectives and the aims of education mentioned above; and conflict between these could exist. Yet it need not be total, for if achievement is wisely assessed it is the logical outcome of an educational process — but this is not to suggest that it is the only outcome. It depends on whether teachers justify what they are doing in school only on utilitarian grounds or in terms of intrinsic worthwhileness. Exam success as an end in itself may motivate pupils but emphasis on it may not give the necessary educational basis to the transaction. On the other hand, as an end it may be the initial means of catching a pupil's interest and so involving him actively in a transaction which is aimed at developing far more than this. Teachers who succeed in gaining a response from pupils, even though some of what is given is rejected and some not fully grasped, can yet help them to catch their concern for what they are transmitting. Such a concern has important relevance for any aim of education; it comes, says Peters (1965, p. 60), from being active in 'some art, attitude or form of thought' and is evidence of a single-mindedness and engagement in what is being shared by teacher and taught. Such engagement in the educational process involves the affective side of a pupil's life and the need for it suggests that the aims of education must include the achievement of not only rational autonomy but also a capacity to feel deeply. Such a capacity implies not only the need for the education of the emotions but for the opportunity to harness both the intellectual and feeling sides of man's life to the pursuit of some worthwhile activity.

This two-fold aim of education implies that, as a result of acquiring a capacity to make rational judgments, an educated person uses not only an intellectual awareness of the knowledge relevant to the particular situation but also concern for it and sensitivity to its worth. Such an aim stresses the interpersonal element in education, and the necessity for active engagement in it. So it is not surprising that writers with very differing approaches to education yet share this concern for the emotional as well as the intellectual side of man's life. Illich, for example, in *De-schooling Society* (1971, p. 17), whilst arguing that much of what is learnt in school is forgotten and not relevant, yet says of education as opposed to schooling that:

> It relies on the *relationship between partners* who already have some of the keys which give access to memories stored in and by the community. . . .
> It relies on the surprise of the unexpected question which opens new doors for the enquirer and his partner.

Likewise, R. S. Peters (1965, p. 62) says:

> Perhaps the greatest educators are those who can convey insensibly the sense of quality in these activities so that a glimmering of what is intrinsic is constantly intimated. The result is that others are drawn along with them to join in the shared experience of exploring a different level of life.

If such experiences are educational and lead in the end to an educated person then our aims of education must have to do with the achieving of certain qualities of mind, and certain attitudes and feelings. Of these William Walsh quoted by L. A. Reid (1962, p. 162) comments, using the language of poet and literary critic, that when we finish our education we discard much of the truck learnt in school. And

> what lasts and what enters into our being as a result of school and college is a blend of value, attitude and assumption, a certain moral tone, a special quality of imagination, a particular flavor of sensibility — the things that constituted the soul of our education.

Further reading

A clear statement of R. S. Peters's view is in *Authority, Responsibility and Education*, Allen & Unwin, 1973. He discusses his views with two others, J. Woods and W. H. Dray, in the chapter 'Aims of Education — a Conceptual Inquiry in Philosophy of Education', in *Philosophy of Education* ed. R. S. Peters, Oxford University Press, 1973.
    R. Pring's article, 'Objectives and innovation: the irrelevance of theory', *London Education Review,* vol. 2, no. 3, Autumn 1973, and I. Illich's book *De-schooling Society,* Open Forum, Penguin, 1971, are both worth reading and will bring out some of the main objections to R. S. Peters's view. A later development in R. S. Peters's thinking can be seen in his article 'Education and the Educated Man', in *Education and the Development of Reason,* Routledge & Kegan Paul, 1972.

P. J. Higginbotham

Bibliography

ILLICH, I. D. (1971), *De-schooling Society*, Open Forum, Penguin.
PETERS, R. S. (1963), *Education as Initiation*, Evans.
PETERS, R. S. (1965), *Ethics and Education*, Allen & Unwin.
PRING, R. (1973), 'Objectives and innovation: the irrelevance of theory', *London Educational Review*, vol. 2, no. 3, Autumn.
REID, L. A. (1962), *Philosophy and Education*, Heinemann.

Chapter five

Knowledge and education

D.I.Lloyd

One feature of our society stands out with particular prominence. It is the challenge offered to our ideas, beliefs, values and views, hitherto accepted, to justify themselves. Institutions like the family, the church and education have had to face the shock of those who have questioned their worth. In a way, such a jolt is welcome. It exposes the staleness into which those institutions can slip that have been satisfied for too long with the same pattern.

In universities and college, students have challenged the decisions of their teachers and the content of their courses. In schools alterations in the authority structure have been attempted with some success. Pupils have pressed for a more democratic system and a greater involvement in making decisions.

In society at large, the opinions of the experts, the mature, the experienced have not been accepted blindly or regarded with the same respect as they were previously. It is felt that none of us is any better than anyone else at saying what is true or should be done.

Why has there been this move? There is no single answer, no simple explanation. Yet, one can see one point of view which lies behind the changes described above. It is the view that the existence of knowledge is not possible. For knowledge of what there is, if it were at all possible, would be unchanging, stable and certain. But individuals, their views, situations and times change so that any such knowledge, it is argued, is plainly impossible. The existence of any objective standards of truth is an illusion. Our understanding of things is always subjective, personal and prone to prejudice. To hanker after anything more 'objective' is to be doomed to disappointment.

In this chapter I want to look more closely at this particular point of view and its alternatives. The reason for this is that unless the strong contemporary challenge concerning the objectivity of knowledge is met then education can never be anything more than persuasion.

D. I. Lloyd

Can there be knowledge?

If someone boasted that he had been educated but knew nothing we would wonder what sort of an education he had had. We might even say that he had wasted his time and his money, for there is at least one thing that he should have got from his education, and that is knowledge. That is, we seem to connect the idea of education with knowledge, and so we are reluctant to say such a person could have been educated. But to speak of knowledge in this way assumes there is such a thing. It is this assumption I want to examine, though at first sight, to do so may seem too ridiculous for words. The question then is: Can there be knowledge? A hasty reply — 'Of course there is!' — really misses the point of the question. For, if we are uncertain whether there can be knowledge, then it makes that teaching which tries to get children to know something a rather pointless business. It would mean that we would never be sure when they were confused or when they had understood or when they had moved from ignorance to knowledge. So, a negative answer to the question, Can there be knowledge?, really would make it impossible for there to be an education system at all. But surely, it might be said, what about the vast knowledge that scientists, mathematicians and historians have accumulated? Is not that knowledge?

I'm afraid we must not be put off by such a reaction. At one time, many people believed in witches, many believed that mad people were evil, and many that the earth was flat. Today we would question those beliefs. So the fact that many people hold certain beliefs, and work by a particular assumption (in our case that there is knowledge), is not enough for us to regard what they say as true. The only way we should be convinced is by the reason or argument that is offered to support that view. So, we must persist with the question, Can there be knowledge?

In order to grasp fully this and other questions in philosophy it is essential to find out why people held the views they did, however unusual or even foolish they seem to us now. The history of our present question dates back, as far as we know, to 500 BC. There was a group of Greek thinkers, called Sophists, who felt that because there could not be knowledge, all you should do in education and life was to talk people into doing what you wanted, i.e. get your own way, which is a somewhat selfish outlook, and shows how a philosophical idea may have practical consequences.

What was their argument — an argument whose echo can be heard these days in the views of certain contemporary sociologists? It runs as follows:

We usually regard our senses as providing us with knowledge. We encourage children to find out things for themselves, the colours of butterflies, the relation between a machine's size and speed, the height of buildings, the path of a stream. Yet at the same time we emphasise how individual we are as people. Our hereditary features are different and our backgrounds are varied. There are no two people who are alike. It is then easy to conclude that we will each see the world from our own standpoint. We can see this writ large in the case of the man suffering from yellow jaundice. He sees the world tinted with yellow because of *his* differences, in this case the effects of yellow jaundice. It so happens that we can find this out in his case. But there is no reason why it should not be true of all of us. As far as we know, when you see red, I see pink, not to say green. It is only that we conveniently have kept on using the same words.

Even within our *own* visual experience a coin can look round, elliptical or even a straight line. And as for the illusions of magicians, hallucinations, these all point to one thing. They point to the unreliability of our senses. Yes, of course something goes on in our heads, of course we believe we are seeing what is there, but, runs the argument, we have no real way of distinguishing what is correct from what is incorrect, what I have seen from what I imagined. All we really can say is that we live in our own private worlds, with only apparent knowledge of an outside world, only having apparent communication with other people.

Language is of little help in overcoming this, as our interpretation of language is personal and individual. And here we have a second argument which is seen to support the sceptic's view. The word 'home', for example, conjures up in our minds quite different images — a warm hearth and an affectionate mother, or central heating and an authoritarian father. Words create different images in our minds. Again, 'democracy' is a word which conveys servility to the tyrant, inefficiency to the totalitarian, the ideal state to the democrat. And there is no shortage of other words which could be cited: good, truth, progress; these can be interpreted in a variety of ways. They mean different things to different people, so that communication is not really possible.

Both these arguments, i.e. the denial of knowledge of physical things and the denial of common meanings, share the view that there are no such things as external standards of what is correct and incorrect, right and wrong, or even better and worse. They are, that is to say, sceptical in character. So that neither a colour chart nor a dictionary would be of any use, for the experiences of these, too, will be interpreted privately, and so differently.

If the sceptic is right then our pursuit of knowledge is pointless, and our attempt at trying to teach someone something is energy wasted.

Let us now examine this argument. One way in philosophy of showing whether there is any logical fatigue in the structure of the argument is to accept temporarily the conclusions of the argument and press them as far as we can, and this we shall do here.

D. I. Lloyd

So first, why, in perception, do we stop at asking if we see the same colour? Perhaps we do not even see the same shapes. What is square to you is rectangular to me, and what is cubic to you is spherical to me.

Why, too, stop at the sense of sight? We may hear different things. What is discordant to you is harmonious to me. We may even taste, smell and feel things differently.

But the argument may be pressed into the world of the person himself. For my own bodily state today is different, however little, from what it was yesterday. So what was smooth to me then may now appear a little coarse. So that not only, on this argument, do we have to say that we do not know who is right between people, but that we do not know which of our own senses is right.

It now looks as if we are in an unusually difficult position, viz., we cannot now distinguish from our own point of view whether we see the same colour, shape and so on. This must in turn mean that we cannot even speak of the same objects, and what they are like for the whole world becomes one of fleeting sensations, a world all confused.

Second, in the case of language, we end up not just in an implausible or uncomfortable position, but an impossible one.

If the sceptic says 'I cannot really know what you mean,' then the most devastating reply to him is 'Pardon?' One often finds these days similar arguments where people are attempting to utter a truth which they do not want to apply to themselves. They are presupposing what they are trying to deny. The situation is like someone who telephones you to say that the line is not working. If he says there is no such thing as truth, he really is sawing off the branch he is sitting on, for he has just uttered what he considers to be a truth. Anyone, then, who says we cannot know what another person means is *conveying* to us at that same time what he himself means. Does not his own attempt to persuade by reason assume that there is a common meaning between himself and others?

At this point you may feel cheated. The problem was posed and you find now that it was not really a problem. You still, in spite of being forced to accept the conclusion, hanker after the original view. In a way that is not surprising for if it is true that the error of your reasoning consists in disbelieving something which you cannot help but believe, then in a way you are not going to learn anything new. Someone expressed the task of philosophy as one of dissolving problems rather than solving them. You may now feel that you are witness to a vanishing trick, a sleight of hand that makes you feel you have been deceived. Whereas in fact, you yourself, if you held the above view, were the arch deceiver when you announced, not that you were going to make *something* vanish, but rather, *everything,* and that taken literally means the magician (yourself) and the audience. But just as something can only disappear as long as something remains visible, so too misunderstanding, being unable to grasp the meaning of another's remarks, is only possible if we understand some things he is saying. To deny then the existence of standards of correctness in our senses and the possibility of grasping the meaning of another's words is absurd as it must apply as well to those very arguments.

Even though you may have been convinced that the outright denial of the existence of knowledge is impossible you may not be prepared to agree that there is definite knowledge. A view you may wish to adopt is the following. Knowledge is possible but it is not easy to obtain. It is somewhat elusive. Whilst in the case of perception, I can never get at what an object looks like exactly, I can at least get near to it. And in the case of language, I can approximate, but only approximate, to the meaning of another person's words. Where people do not know each other very well, it is argued, the communication gap between them is great, but between friends the gap is much smaller. Yet there is always a gap, something which cannot be conveyed to the other.

In reply, we must ask how, if I cannot get absolutely clear what someone is saying on some occasions, I can say that on other occasions I am either near or far from achieving that. How could I find this out? How can we tell even with friends whether we are understanding or misunderstanding each other? Imagine my trying to guess the length of a stick in your pocket. I might guess at first that it is 10 cms long, then 15 cms. Now if I never had the chance to see what it really looked like, how could one say whether I had made a good guess or not? Likewise if your meaning is enclosed within you, never openly accessible, always behind closed doors, how could I ever say whether any attempt to understand you was succeeding? It would, of course, be no help for you to tell me how I was getting on, for as in our examination of the previous argument, that itself would be subject to the same misunderstandings as you were trying to correct in me. So that this argument, too, generates its own fatal disease.

A third argument which is different from either denying the existence of knowledge or saying that we can only approximate to it, is that which says that if a person believes he is right, he is right for himself. When I challenge the view of another I would be told that we are entitled to our own points of view. You think what you do, and I think what I do. We each have a right to what we think and what we each think is right. To challenge the rightness of another person's point of view is to manifest an excess of dogmatism and a lack of tolerance.

I have heard this view put forward by young children, students and others. It has something appealing about it. First, it points to the fact that many of the things we have taken on trust from our parents can and must be challenged. The views they imparted to us as absolute we may have found to be not so. We were told never to tell untruths, but we are made to see that occasions, when, for instance, a person has an incurable disease, it may be right to mislead because we care for them so much, and know they cannot bear the truth. Second, we have learned how other people live differently from ourselves, and we feel that it would be both insensitive and unfair to regard them as mistaken. Perhaps the most obvious case for this argument is where opinion seems to be as a matter of taste, as in clothes, food, furniture, hair style, as well as in painting, music and drama. What we like is a personal matter. It is linked with our personality, the kind of person we are, so the argument goes. We may comment on the clothes of another as being unusual, way out, or unconventional, but we do not say they are wrong. In food, some like sweet things, others savoury. A menu is designed to cater for different tastes and there is no question of there being a correct choice. It is a matter of preference. In this sphere as in all others, it is argued, it is a personal matter.

I do not wish to argue against this view of taste but to the view in its general form. Let me start in the area of morals. There are people who agree with vivisection, others who are against the practice; some for abortion, others not; some support the family, others see it as outmoded; some see capital punishment as effective whilst others see it as inhuman. Here I have mentioned some controversial cases but it would be misleading to take controversial cases as a basis on which to argue the question of rightness or wrongness. Let us take a non-controversial case. Mugging, the recent practice of beating up defenceless people, either young children or the aged, may be seen by those that practise it as 'O.K. for a laugh'. Do we want to say in this case, not only that they are entitled to their own opinion but that they are right if that is what they think? Another example: a child steals from the coats of other children their money, sweets and books. When asked why he does it he replies that he 'just wanted them'. That is certainly his view and he is absolutely right in saying it is his view, i.e. he is reporting it correctly, but it is a further question whether his view is correct. These two views, it seems to me, are not controversial in character, but are clearly wrong and furthermore, we should help children to see why they are wrong.

If the moral case is not sufficiently convincing, then let us take the case where someone denies that the date is, say 25 December. Would we say, in this case, that he is right for himself? If we do, then we have to make the following rather ridiculous statement about the person's belief – 'I think it is 25 December, I have checked the calendar, everyone is eating turkey, children are playing with their new toys, Scrooge is smiling, but I also think he is right for himself even though he is wrong.' Surely, both he and I cannot be right. The date is either 25 December or it is not. Here then is no room for doubt. I agree this does not mean that all matters of fact are like this. What the facts are in Northern Ireland or any emotionally charged situation is, of course, difficult to establish, but even that does not prove that it is still a matter of personal opinion, only that it is difficult to find out the facts. I would want to argue the same for the moral case, that some things are clearly examples of meanness or generosity. Supporting one's case must in the end be done by citing examples of the kind I have mentioned.

So this third view, which has the flavour of tolerance, is deceptive. In accepting everything as a legitimate point of view it must accept the possibility of someone's regarding bullying as a virtue and heroism as a vice. One cannot conceive of any world which could hold such values. It seems to me unintelligible and incoherent and that is the argument against it.

The aim of this section has been to establish that any view which denies the existence of knowledge is self-defeating. If that view is mistaken, then it must be true that knowledge does exist, and this is, if we link knowledge with education, an important step. The next stage in the argument is to indicate briefly what knowledge consists of.

What does knowledge consist of?

What we now have to consider is the kind of things we can understand and know. In chapter 6 we shall look closely at what has been called the structure of knowledge, and the character which anything which has a claim to knowledge should possess. In the rest of this section we shall look briefly at this area before its more systematic treatment.

In philosophy, there have been two main, but opposing answers to the question concerning the *nature* of knowledge. One view has been that we can only have knowledge when we allow our reason to work on its own, unhindered by those senses we spoke of earlier, which provide us with unreliable, inconsistent information. But what, you may ask, could we know if we ignored what our senses tell us? One subject of knowledge that would qualify would be mathematics, in contrast with science which has to do with observation. Mathematics involves reasoning which has little or nothing to do with our senses. This can be shown by the fact that a sum like $7 + 5 = 12$ (base 10) is always true. No information from our senses could serve either to confirm it or disprove it. If a child said he found it made 13, we would not think he had found something new, but that he had made a mistake. Yet, if a child told us he had found the oldest tombstone in the churchyard was 250 years old, we might want to say he was either right or wrong. But to answer him, we would have to find out and see for ourselves — on this view a method thought to be unreliable. In the case of mathematics the certainty here is definite and absolute. Surely, here we have the model of knowledge, something that is unchangeable.

Other philosophers took an opposite position. They saw the permanence of this so-called knowledge and its independence of the world around us being its weakness rather than its strength. It was, so to speak, so heavenly that it was no earthly good. (Modern philosophers have spoken of the statements which make up this kind of knowledge as being trivially true.) They want to argue that the only source of knowledge is experience which is acquired through the use of our senses. Science, for example, and its various branches, constitute this knowledge.

Clearly then, the content of a school curriculum would be very different depending upon one's view of knowledge. Plato, in *The Republic* suggests a curriculum consisting of mathematics and philosophy for those who will rule, for these are two subjects which he says are rational and non-scientific in their nature. For Plato this view of mathematics is linked with his view of the soul and the body. He saw the soul (psyche) of man as having an unhealthy acquaintance with the body. The soul's true activity is to reason, the body to sense, and so, where possible, we should cut ourselves off from the body, or at least counteract its corruptible activities.

Few philosophers take up either position exclusively. One philosophical argument which opposes the polarisation of the above views contends that we should look for distinctive features of knowledge in particular areas rather than find a common measure to which all subjects must conform. So that one would today find both mathematics and science on the school timetable. Both subjects and those like them are regarded as having a contribution to that knowledge which will have a different character when its material is different.

Are we then agreed these days about the content of the school curriculum? Your visits to school and your experience will show differing points of view. Some subjects are regarded, in comparison with subjects like science, as having no value, little value, or an equal value. Art, for example, is excluded on the grounds that it is a luxury we can ill afford, or looked on as a subject which has little merit except for infants, for whom it is an outlet for inner conflicts, or rated as a subject which can stand on its own feet without embarrassment alongside the so-called respectable subjects. A teacher then needs to be persuaded that a subject is eligible for inclusion.

Another case is religion. An increasing number of people argue that we should not teach religious education as a subject in school and certainly not as a compulsory subject. They argue (1) that many religious statements are not supported by evidence, that is, the no-one-has-ever-come-back-and-told-us argument; (2) that religious statements are plainly false, i.e. 'God is good' is false because of the evil that exists in the world which contradicts that statement; or (3) that statements like 'God is Our Father' are meaningless. They have no sense because when we try and describe what kind of a Father He is we are forced to give the word a meaning more and more removed from the world. We say He is not older, He has no body, eats no food — what then could we mean by calling Him a father? On the other hand those who want to argue that RE should be included, differ amongst themselves in the arguments they offer. Some use logical arguments that God exists and others empirical arguments. The former attempt to prove that there could not be a world without God and the latter claim that, just as people have experience of the presence and love of other people, so they have experience of the presence and love of God; and there is no shortage of such people.

A claim that there is moral knowledge is in some ways more problematic. First, there is the problem of disagreement. We have our own personal views about abortion, punishment, segregation, public schools and the family. So we have to try and understand whether it is proper to speak of being right and wrong in morals — and, if so, how do we know we are right? But in education we also have the problem of how, if at all, we can enable people to acquire this knowledge. For unlike PE, which you can timetable in the hall after break on Mondays, moral understanding does not lend itself to easy planning. There are many reasons for this which lend themselves to fruitful discussion. An important one is that when we have dealings with other people, our dealings are in a moral climate. Morality is the backcloth against which we think, speak and act. So a teacher may either ignore or take account of a child's request to have a turn on the wall bars. A teacher may laugh at, correct, punish, or make an example of a boy who has been copying in mathematics. A teacher may show gratitude to or deride a girl who has helped a newcomer to the class. These examples point to the fact that we are continually behaving in a moral way towards those we teach. Here, then, we have not only the fact that there may be such a thing as moral knowledge, but that if there is such a thing we are inescapably involved in both its transmission and application.

These are just some of the problems that are connected with the question of what knowledge consists of. Further examination of the curriculum would be needed to establish whether any subjects are more important than others, as well as how they differ from one another. It is often surprising how few students are able to make a case for the inclusion of their subject on the curriculum. An inability to do so makes one an easy prey for those who would wish to exclude it.

In these two sections we have raised the question of the possibility of knowledge and the forms it might take. We have argued that knowledge is a logical inevitability by showing that any attempt to say anything implies its existence. Over what constitutes knowledge people often differ, though there is a good deal of agreement. The epistemological credentials of science are rarely questioned whereas those of morals are frequently being challenged.

The discussion is by no means over in either of the two areas dealt with above. Contemporary writings by sociologists on the nature of knowledge demand closer examination, and clarification of the nature of different subjects has not been fully achieved. The aim of this chapter has been to indicate how such problems might be solved; and also, for some, that there are such problems.

Further reading

The linking of education with knowledge can be seen in most of R. S. Peters's writings. See for example *Ethics and Education,* Allen & Unwin, 1965, ch. 2.

A readable account and critique of the range of sceptical views of knowledge can be found in D. W. Hamlyn's *Theory of Knowledge,* Macmillan, 1971, ch. 2.

One particular subject which raises important questions concerning its status as knowledge and whether it should be taught in school is religion. A lively discussion of this issue can be found in the following articles: P. H. Hirst, 'Morals, religion in the maintained school', *British Journal of Educational Studies,* vol. XIV, 1965–6; D. Z. Phillips, 'Philosophy and religious education', *British Journal of Educational Studies,* vol. XVIII, 1970; P. H. Hirst, 'Philosophy and religious education. A reply to D. Z. Phillips', *British Journal of Educational Studies,* vol. XVIII, 1970.

A helpful book in the study of ethics is J. Hospers's *Human Conduct,* Hart-Davis, 1961.

Chapter six

Forms of knowledge

D.S.Wringe

In chapter 5 an attempt was made to show that knowledge is possible and that claims that it is not really do not make sense. Then follows a brief account of two opposing philosophical views about the nature of knowledge and the debate which has taken place over the centuries about the kinds of things we can know with greatest certainty. At the end of the chapter we are shown how our views about what counts as genuine knowledge must, if we think them through, affect the way we would plan the school curriculum.

In this chapter and the next we must now press some of these enquiries further. You may have been persuaded by the kind of argument which was advanced earlier against the sceptic. You may now agree with him, if you did not before, that if a person says 'There is no such thing as truth' and yet regards his own utterances as true, this is extremely inconsistent of him. But you may still be feeling rather puzzled about how it is possible to distinguish statements which are true from those which are not, about how many true statements there are, about whether there are different kinds of true statements and so on.

Which statements can we call true?

If you are persuaded that the word 'true' is meaningful, that we cannot do without the notion of truth if we are to communicate at all, you may still not understand on what grounds we feel entitled to apply the term 'true' to some statements rather than to others.

Let us take some examples. Most people would agree that the following are true statements and that it would be perfectly proper for pupils to learn these in school.

(a) (i) The Great Fire of London took place in 1666.
    (ii) Paris is the capital of France.

    (iii) Edelweiss are found in the Swiss Alps.

    (iv) The inhabitants of Belgium speak either French or Flemish.

    (v) Shakespeare wrote a number of well known plays.

We can contrast these with statements over which it seems more difficult to reach agreement. This is not just because we do not yet know whether or not there is a Loch Ness monster, for example, or whether the world will end with a bang or a whimper. It is because it is less clear how to obtain agreement about the truth of a statement like:

(b) (i) Shakespeare is a greater playwright than Racine.

    (ii) Britain's withdrawal from India represented a great act of British statesmanship.

It seems even experts can differ about statements like these without necessarily losing their reputation for telling the truth.

Then there are statements like:

(c) (i) 'It is better to travel hopefully than to arrive and the true success is to labour' (Stevenson).

    (ii) 'Il faut cultiver son jardin' (Voltaire), which might be translated as 'We must get on with the work in hand.'

About these there is inevitably disagreement amongst experts and others just because people have, and seem to have a right to have, different views about how it is best to lead one's life. Is there any way in which issues like these might be resolved?

Finally there are statements which some people seriously claim not to be able to assess as true or false because they say they do not even know what they mean.

Examples would include statements made about works of art such as:

(d) (i) Gauguin's painting presents us with answers to the questions 'Where have we come from?', 'What are we?', 'Where are we going?'

or religious statements like:

    (ii) The emotion which it is appropriate to experience during an act of worship is awe.

Now, if you had previously thought that in education we could simply divide off those statements which most people would agree to be true from those which they agree to be false or from those about which there is controversy and simply teach the former, I hope that you can see that things are not quite as easy as that.

In the first place we may be mistaken about those very statements which we now regard as most certainly true. After all people once thought and taught that the world was flat. To what extent did they advance their children's education?

Second, if we omit all mention of those statements like class (b), that is statements which contain an evaluative element and are controversial even among scholars, we shall be unlikely to educate pupils to the point where some of them go on to settle once and for all where the truth lies. In other words, we shall be unlikely to produce future scholars able themselves to contribute to human knowledge.

Third, statements like class (c), about which there appears to be general disagreement, and not just among experts, may be rather more important to us than safe but trivial statements like, for example, the fact that it rained in Bromley on 8 May 1973. So once again, it seems, a consideration of statements like these, though they are controversial, might be legitimately defended for inclusion in an educational programme.

Finally, if those statements which some people claim they cannot understand and therefore cannot regard as true or false can be successfully defended as meaningful and true, then they represent various kinds of knowledge – for example religious and aesthetic knowledge (class (d)) which just because they are forms of knowledge cannot be lightly omitted from children's education.

Now, the examples I have discussed are intended to indicate some of the further issues which arise once it has been admitted that the word 'true' is meaningful and that knowledge at least in some cases is possible.

But surely, you may feel like protesting, teachers, even less student-teachers, cannot be expected to sort out the wheat from the chaff in these matters. They cannot reasonably be expected to distinguish what is true and important from what is uncertain or trivial.

In the first place teachers are far too busy thinking how to teach their pupils or even *what* to teach them within a limited area. Second, the human race is accumulating knowledge at such a rate that they would scarcely know where to begin. Third, it is doubtful whether without some kind of framework within which to work teachers could even start to do this. It is after all a mammoth task to list and classify all those statements which because they are controversial and important ought to be taught or introduced to children during their time in school.

Nevertheless, it seems that, in spite of these difficulties, teachers and students ought to be aware not only of difficulties arising out of arguments about the *possibility* of knowledge but also that this problem is related to the further question of the kind of justification which can be given for regarding various *different* kinds of statement as true. They should also want to know how to answer the question 'How *many* different kinds of true statement are there?' It is to these problems that we shall now turn in the next section.

How many different kinds of true statement are there?

If we refer back to the section in chapter 2 where the two traditional views about what is the best or perhaps the only kind of justification for claiming that a statement is true were discussed you will remember that over the centuries some philosophers have thought that only statements based on our sense experiences of the material world can legitimately be regarded as true. Others have thought we can be more certain about truths of reason, as in logic or mathematics. In my original examples, the first set (a) are all based in some way on our experience of the universe and its contents.

But it is also possible to contrast both these kinds of true statement with those whose truth we may accept depending on how far we are satisfied with the kind of case that can be made out for them *in some quite different way*. Such candidates would include the historical and aesthetic judgments included in category (b), the views about how it is best to lead one's life in category (c) and the aesthetic and religious statements in category (d) which are intended to be informative about the meaning of the picture in question, about the nature of religious experience and so on.

But is it possible, you will want to ask — and this is the crux of the matter — to apply the term 'true' to *all* or indeed to *any* of the statements in categories (b), (c), (d). If it is, what sort of case can be made out for doing so?

Well, we can certainly approach the problem by saying what kind of argument will not do. If statements like those included under (b), (c) and (d) are true it is certainly *not* because somebody in authority says so. Thus if an 'expert' declares that Shakespeare is a greater writer than Racine it is open to us to ask on what grounds this is being asserted. The reply 'Because I say so', no matter how eminent the author of the remarks, is unlikely to satisfy us unless he goes on to tell us the reasons *why* he says so.

Second, if statements like those under (b), (c) and (d) are true it is not because *most people* think that they are. We cannot settle any of these issues by taking a show of hands. Of course in the television programme 'Opportunity Knocks' the question as to who is the most talented performer is settled in terms of the number of votes recorded, but it would be clearly absurd to settle the relative merits of Racine and Shakespeare in this way, and even more so to decide the truth of statements like 'Britain's withdrawal from India represented a great act of British statesmanship' or 'Gauguin's painting presents us with answers to the questions "Where have we come from?", "What are we?", "Where are we going?" ' by getting large numbers of people to fill in yes/no answers in a questionnaire.

Third, we cannot settle the truth of statements like those under discussion by reference to our own private experiences. Someone might try to argue that 'It is better to travel hopefully than to arrive and the true success is to labour' because he had always found it so from experience. But a person is only entitled to state what he has found preferable *for him* from experience. He cannot go on to argue, on this basis alone, that his preference should be allowed to dictate a general policy — unless of course he believes one of two things. Either he might think that he is entitled to prescribe policies for other people even if they do feel quite differently from him, on the basis of his experience *alone,* which seems unreasonable. Alternatively he might naïvely assume that everybody simply does have the same experience as he does — in which case this would need to be factually established before he was entitled to formulate a policy based on this assumption.

So far we have proceeded only negatively. We are still left with the problem of whether it is possible to make a case for applying the term 'true' to statements like some of those included under (b), (c) and (d), that is to statements which are neither mathematical truths nor truths based on our sense experiences.

In order to see whether we can do this I propose to reclassify the statements under (b), (c) and (d). I shall use categories like 'historical', 'aesthetic', 'religious', 'ethical' and so on — categories which, in fact, overlap those of my original classification. I shall do this because attempts to say that we *can* extend the number of statements to which we are justified in applying the term 'true' most frequently use this kind of categorisation. Certainly one of the most important attempts to argue that it *is* possible to regard other statements as true besides mathematical or scientific statements is framed in this way. I refer, of course, to the view that there are a *number* of distinct forms of knowledge, as put forward by Hirst.

Now before I go on to elaborate and discuss his account I wish to illustrate by looking at a particular example how it might be possible to argue that statements can be known as true in a way different from the truths of mathematics and science. I have chosen history, partly because there have been attempts from time to time to defend history as a kind of imperfect science. But I have also chosen it because there has already been in chapter 2, some discussion of the problems relating to the possibility of religious and moral knowledge which are, of course, two equally controversial areas.

The case of historical statements

The nature of historical statements and the kind of case we can make in defence of their being true has long been a matter of dispute. Sometimes, as I have said, there have been attempts to see history as a rather imperfect science. On this view truly historical statements are about events such as the Great Fire of London for which there is both evidence of the senses, for example the account given in Pepys's diary which we can read, and for which explanations can be given. These explanations are analogous to the kind of explanation we give of scientific events. Thus we say Mr Jones's water pipes burst because the water in them froze and water expands when it freezes. Similarly the Great Fire of London took place because the conditions under which fires generally take place were fulfilled on this occasion.

But there are at least two good reasons why we should not regard historical statements as similar to scientific statements. In the first place the kind of evidence which is available to our senses has to be interpreted if it is to be *historical* evidence. In other words it has to be 'read' in a certain way which is particular to history. This is true both of accounts of the time like Pepys's diary, and of archaeological finds. I shall return to this point presently.

Second, although historical events like the Great Fire of London *can* be explained as if they were no more than scientific events — they are also the outcome of human actions which may well not be susceptible of the same kind of explanation. Consider for example the 'event' of Henry VIII's marriage to Anne Boleyn.

We may contrast this approach to history with the view which holds that the business of acquiring historical knowledge is that of trying to understand the way men, both important and unimportant, lived their lives in a previous age. Now to understand this is to understand how *they* saw the world they lived in, how *they* saw their institutions. It is to see their actions from *their* point of view.

According to Isaiah Berlin, Vico, an eighteenth-century philosopher, was close to discovering the nature of historical activity (Berlin, 1972). He understood that this kind of understanding *presupposes* an understanding of human nature and that this is quite a different matter from understanding the subject-matter of science — that is the natural objects in the universe.

And when we ask why particular men in the past acted as they did, why a particular society or nation reacted as it did to a particular event in its history, say a natural disaster, or conquest, we can answer this at a different level from that at which we explain the behaviour of rocks or animals, whose inner workings we cannot claim to understand. Indeed, we cannot even tell whether it makes sense to speak of 'inner' in their case — of motives, wishes, fears, hopes: generally we assume that it does not.

We understand what it is to have purposes, to strive, to act, because we know what it is to be a human being. We know what it is to want, to fear, to hope, to imagine, to worship, to conceive an ideal, and we know this in a way different from that in which we know that blue is different from green, or that rocks have certain properties which trees do not have, or the way in which we know logical truths: for instance, that certain propositions are and some are not compatible with each other. We know what moves man and how, because it is part of human experience.

Vico's importance was that he thought there were two key ways into understanding those who lived in a different age from our own. One was by understanding their language; another was by understanding the significance of their rituals and myths. To elaborate Vico's point about language, Berlin claims that if the ancients, for example, appear to use language rather differently from the way we use it, it may be that their usage is to be taken literally.

When the ancients say that 'the blood boils in my breast', may it not be, Vico wonders, that the sensation of anger seemed to them literally more like blood boiling than it now seems to us? When they used expressions like 'lips of vases', 'teeth of ploughs', 'mouths of rivers', 'necks of land', 'veins of minerals', 'bowels of the earth' — to take only metaphors drawn from the human body — Vico suggests that they saw vases as having lips, ploughs as having teeth, in much more vivid and concrete terms than any in which we, in our sophisticated way, can conceive these things. These are dead metaphors now. But for our ancestors rivers had mouths, land had necks, oaks had hearts, minerals had veins and the earth had bowels. For early man the willows wept much more than they weep for us, and all these modes of speech have turned into clichés.

Equally important for Vico was the significance of ritual and myth. This latter point has been endorsed in recent times by Winch's remarks about the way in which we are required to extend our imagination if we are to understand a contemporary primitive society (Winch, 1958).

On this kind of account, then, historical events are no longer simply happenings with a cause or causes like scientific events. They are at least partly the outcome of human actions, and the situations which arose in the past are situations in which people participated both wittingly and unwittingly — which they perceived in a certain way and responded to accordingly, in a way governed by their existing beliefs, traditions and so on. Seen in this way the Great Fire of London becomes quite a different kind of phenomenon from, say, a highly Americanised film of it. On this view, too, historical understanding has been achieved when we are able to understand how a situation which today strikes *us* as quite extraordinary seemed absolutely normal to people living at the time. It takes quite a lot of imagination to enter into the thinking of people who seriously believed the earth to be flat, for example.

It would of course be a mistake to think that the historian has *only* to enter the minds of those who lived in the past. For just as people on the outside of situations in which other people are involved can detect motives where those who are involved may be guilty of self-deception, or may understand better than those involved the processes of social inter-action at work in a situation, so historians bring to their understanding of past situations a greater objectivity than either was, or even could *in principle* have been, achieved at the time.

It is hoped that it can be seen from this account that it is a difficult matter to ascertain the exact nature of historical statements and the kinds of evidence which entitle historians to claim that their statements are indeed true. But at least it may now be clear why the evidence which historians submit is not the *same* as that which scientists submit in defence of their statements about the universe and its contents.

You may also be able to see now why some philosophers would be inclined to incorporate historical understanding within a more broadly defined area to do with the understanding of minds – our own and other people's.

I hope I have shown the kind of case which can be made out for regarding historical knowledge as a perfectly legitimate form of know-ledge in its own right – a form of knowledge which may bear affinities to other kinds of knowledge but which is nevertheless importantly different from these other kinds.

But as I said earlier, teachers need to know something about the *number* of forms of knowledge for which a case can be made. It is for this reason that I turn now to consider in more detail Hirst's account which gives an overall description of the forms of knowledge and attempts to pick out what their general features are.

The forms of knowledge view

No theory appears suddenly out of thin air. This is true both of the view that there are a number of distinct forms of knowledge and that this fact is educationally significant. But Hirst's account is perhaps one of the most important attempts to relate systematically the various kinds of contribution which are relevant to this enterprise.

As recently as 1936 Ayer had tried to show that only statements based on sense experience can really be called true at all and that all other statements must either be reduced to statements about our sense experiences or else are meaningless. Indeed he went so far as to write as follows: 'The only information which we can legitimately derive from the study of our own aesthetic and moral experiences is information about our own mental and physical makeup'. By that he meant that when we say that a picture is beautiful we simply mean that we like it. Similarly when we call an action good we merely mean that we are pleased by it.

As you may imagine this kind of view met with considerable opposition, in due course, not only from philosophers who felt that Ayer had not succeeded in his enterprise, but also from scholars who on Ayer's account were simply engaged in either meaningless or mistaken pursuits. Nor were educationists left unmoved by this kind of challenge, for they were left with the job of defending those areas which they felt, perhaps almost intuitively, they ought not to neglect in human life generally, and in children's education in particular.

At the present time we can distinguish three kinds of attempts to clarify forms of knowledge and their significance for education. First, there are those attempts which are, philosophically speaking, part of a highly technical debate — that is, they are attempts by professional philosophers to use philosophical tools to clarify the nature of, for example, material objects, works of art, right actions, so as to defend the possibility of knowledge of these.

Second, we can pick out attempts which are specialised in a different way. They are undertaken by those who are clear that they are in fact engaged in the pursuit and transmission of a particular form of knowledge. They try to give (from the inside of the discipline, as it were) an informed characterisation of what its logical features are. Here one might quote the work of Gardiner 1968 on the nature of history, for example, or the recent attempts of various historians to try to make explicit for teachers and students what they take the features of historical knowledge to be (Rowse *et al.*, 1973).

Third, there have been attempts to pick out and defend in perhaps a rather metaphorical or poetic way those important areas of activity and experience which ought to be transmitted to the next generation.

Cassirer for example wrote: 'No longer in a merely physical universe, man lives in a symbolic universe. Language, myth, art and religion are parts of this universe. They are the varied threads which weave the symbolic net, the tangled web of human experience' (1944, p. 25).

Now accounts like this last one, or that of Oakeshott (1962) or Phenix (1964) for example, stand or fall in terms of their *adequacy* as accounts of the nature and scope of human knowledge, and second, in terms of their *persuasiveness* about the significance of the fact that there are a number of important areas of human experience. If Hirst's account, which I shall now go on to discuss, is to be preferred to these it is precisely because it really is an attempt to come to grips with what for philosophers are fundamental questions, namely 'What do we mean by calling statements true?', 'What is our justification for applying the term "true" to this particular kind of statement?'

Second, it is an attempt to work on a broad front and to sketch in general terms just how many kinds of distinct knowledge there are. Finally, it is an attempt to give the existence of different kinds of knowledge the greatest possible significance for education and for human life generally.

Thus whereas someone like Cassirer was prepared to talk rather vaguely about the various forms of symbolic activity which man has evolved, Hirst tries to distinguish symbolic or meaningful activities from those activities which are, of course, meaningful but which *in addition* are concerned with formulating true statements about the world and our experience of it.

Now this distinction is important because there are some activities like chess which are meaningful in the sense that they are rule-governed and purposive but not, nevertheless, truth-stating activities. The problem, then, is that of distinguishing between activities like chess where people simply make rule-governed moves and activities like doing mathematics where one would want to say people are not only making meaningful rule-governed moves but are also making true statements about the world. So the question is 'How can we pick out just what it is about certain activities which makes them truth-stating rather than simply rule-governed?'

Now one way of doing this would be to see if all the activities which various people allege to be truth-stating share certain features, and if so to try to pick these out. But you can see that it would be difficult to start like this because we might find ourselves having to include things like astrology, and having to omit things like the arts, if we merely went on people's say-so.

Another way of approaching the problem would be to construct a hypothesis about what a form of knowledge is by looking at the features of one or two forms of knowledge which seem to have very wide acceptance. Here a different problem would arise, for if we took mathematics and science as our initial examples (as it would be very tempting to do) and looked into why we consider these to be truth-stating activities we should find, as I have already attempted to show, not only that we had different reasons in each case but also that these are not the same reasons as can be given for regarding history as a truth-stating activity, for example. So this approach might lead us to prejudge seriously the issue about how many forms of knowledge there are, and to end up with a very restricted view of the possible forms of knowledge.

These, then, are two important difficulties facing someone who is attempting, as Hirst is, to pick out those features which a form of knowledge *must* possess if it is to be a form of knowledge and those features which, if they *alone* are present, enable us to claim that we are dealing with a form of knowledge. What then does Hirst say?

First, he claims that wherever there is a form of knowledge there are statements formulated in terms which have a logic or grammar of their own and which thus can only be combined with other similar terms, if what is stated is to make sense. Thus to elaborate this point we *can* say that two plus two equals four. We cannot say that two plus two is sinful. We *can* say that metals expand when heated. We cannot say that the expansion of metals should never be allowed. We *can* say that Henry VIII married Anne Boleyn. We cannot say that events caused Henry VIII's marriage to Anne Boleyn. We *can* say that *Tess of the d'Urbervilles* is a great novel. We cannot say that *Tess of the d'Urbervilles* proves that we are puppets in the hands of the gods.

Next, the statements which can be meaningfully constructed within a form of knowledge are, in some sense, testable against experience. This is to say that they can be asserted as true and that there are publicly agreed ways of testing out their truth, though these may differ, as we have already seen, according to the type of claim that is being made. In other words justifying the truth of a historical statement is very different from justifying the truth of a scientific or mathematical one.

As we have already seen there are further problems regarding the extent to which there *is* public agreement over the possibility of defending the truth of religious, moral and aesthetic statements. But on Hirst's account, whenever there *is* such public agreement about the tests for the truth and falsity of statements then there is a form of knowledge.

Furthermore each form of knowledge has its own way of expressing and testing out the statements it makes. To take an extreme example, within the arts it may be that works of art *themselves* are the true statements of which that particular form is composed. But how different the procedures involved in producing, interpreting and evaluating works of art are from the processes which go on in a science laboratory or on an archaeological site!

In his first article Hirst suggests that there are seven distinct forms of knowledge according to his criteria. In *The Logic of Education* (1970) he still claims that there are seven forms but labels them rather differently. There they are said to be logic and mathematics, the physical sciences, the knowledge of our own and other minds, moral knowledge, aesthetic knowledge, religious knowledge and philosophical knowledge.

All the labels *we* are accustomed to would fit somewhere into this categorisation. Thus knowledge of our own and other minds would include history and the social sciences. Equally the physical sciences would include geology, physics, chemistry, biology, biochemistry and so forth.

We have now probably reached the point where even if you now understand the kind of account Hirst is trying to give of the form of knowledge, you will still want to ask as teachers what the point of the enterprise is. The answer is that on Hirst's account the fact that there are a number of logically distinct forms is important not just because a person's life is richer if he is introduced to one or more of these. Rather, for him, the possibility of a person's having a mind *at all* depends on his being initiated into those forms of knowledge which can be distinguished on his criteria. He says (1969, p. 151):

> Looked at this way, the development of mind has been marked off by the progressive differentiation in human consciousness of some seven (or eight) distinguishable cognitive structures each of which involves the making of a distinctive form of reasoned judgment and is therefore a unique expression of man's rationality.

It is therefore of critical importance to try to assess his account of the forms of knowledge, because of their alleged significance in human life, and it is to this that I shall now turn in the final section.

Difficulties in the forms of knowledge account

Hirst's attempt to distinguish forms of knowledge, it has been argued so far, is of fundamental philosophical and educational significance. Nevertheless his account has been criticised on a number of grounds (Hindess, 1972). In this section an attempt will be made to examine the validity of these criticisms.

First, it has been objected that Hirst does not make clear what is the ultimate status of the forms of knowledge as he distinguishes them, nor even the status of his attempt. To put this point in a different way a recent critic has asked whether the forms of knowledge as distinguished by Hirst are just historical products — that is whether they just happen to have emerged in their present form — or whether they are in fact a categorisation of something timeless and unchangeable for all time. If the former is the case then it is argued Hirst is simply trying to spell out in philosophical terms something which at present is a true description of the facts about knowledge but which may one day no longer be so.

If on the other hand the latter is the case, then Hirst is trying to give us an account of what *must* be the case about knowledge; that is, a description of the facts about the way knowledge is divided up which we could not imagine to be otherwise in any historical circumstances at all.

The only further possibility is that the statement that there are forms of knowledge is neither a statement which is simply true as it happens, like the statement 'The Great Fire of London took place in 1666', nor is it a statement which is true in the same way that 'Two plus two equals four' is true. If it is true then it is true in a way which is importantly different from both of these.

Whether this can be shown remains at present a controversial question. The need however for a fuller and defensible account of just what the status of the theory that there are forms of knowledge *is,* is made clear by the contemporary challenge made by sociologists of knowledge to which reference was made in chapter 2. They want to argue that the basis on which our knowledge is parcelled up and meted out in schools to future generations is at best arbitrary — that is the result of a historical accident. At worst it is held to be the outcome of a plot by the so-called 'middle classes' in whose interest it is held to be to hang on to our present descriptions of the forms of knowledge, *regardless* of whether these are correct. Meanwhile the best way to illustrate further how *particular* forms of knowledge might be shown to be absolute in one sense and in another sense arbitrary, is to consider two examples.

In the area of ethics, for example, it has been suggested (Griffiths, 1957) that the principle of rational benevolence (that is, that the good of others ought to weigh with us as being as important as our own) is, in a sense, necessarily true since if it is not true there is no context in which we can meaningfully raise questions about what we ought to do for the best. Similarly, I should try to argue for aesthetics that if 'It is appropriate to view works of art *as* works of art rather than to collect them as objects of financial value, or to consider them as objects of historical interest' is not true, then there is *no* context within which statements about works of art as such can be made. So the statement is *necessarily* true in the sense that the whole of aesthetic discourse presupposes it. On the other hand, that we have come to evolve modes of discourse which we can characterise as 'ethical' or 'aesthetic' is a historical fact, and one which might have been otherwise.

Another objection to the forms of knowledge approach is that, as has already been stated, throughout Hirst's writings there is considerable variation as to what he takes these to be.

> under the first characterisation 'morals' features in the list of forms of knowledge but not under the second which emphasises testability. There are other discrepancies. Science is separated into physical sciences and human sciences and history together with human sciences get replaced by interpersonal understanding and morals (Hindess, 1972, p. 165).

Further there are discrepancies between his account and that given by Dearden who claims to be using Hirst's work as a basis for his own analysis (Dearden, 1968). What lies behind this objection is presumably the worry that if philosophers were now to address themselves to the question of how many forms of knowledge there are, they might seriously disagree on the matter. But so they do on many of the matters to which they *have* given their concerted attention. To take an obvious case, philosophers who do not for a moment doubt that ethics exists as a subject of study disagree in very important ways about whether we *can* derive statements about what we ought to do from statements about what is the case. So it ought not to surprise us that the questions of how many fundamental forms of knowledge there are and which precisely these are still remains to a certain extent open.

Of course it is an *urgent* question for educationists since they have to concern themselves with the scope of educational curricula and their legitimacy. It is for this reason that, even if it is in some respects provisional, Hirst's analysis *ought* to be of considerable help to curriculum planners. Even so, there is considerable disagreement amongst those who *are* actually interested in planning the curriculum as to how far this account *is* a helpful one. There is also disagreement about what precisely can be inferred from his analysis. The chapter which follows on the curriculum will therefore be designed to concentrate on problems arising in this area.

Further reading

Reference to the forms of knowledge account is to be found in P. H. Hirst, 'Liberal Education and the Nature of Knowledge', in R. D. Archambault (ed.), *Philosophical Analysis and Education*, Routledge & Kegan Paul, 1965; P. H. Hirst, 'Education Theory' in J. W. Tibble (ed.), *The Study of Education*, Routledge & Kegan Paul, 1966; P. H. Hirst, 'The Contribution of Philosophy to the Study of the Curriculum', in J. F. Kerr (ed.), *Changing the Curriculum*, University of London Press, 1968; and P. H. Hirst, 'The logic of the curriculum', *Journal of Curriculum Studies*, vol. 1, no. 2, 1969.

R. F. Dearden, *Philosophy of Primary Education*, Routledge & Kegan Paul, 1968, pp. 64–92, uses a similar analysis. A critique of this account is contained in E. Hindess, 'Forms of knowledge', in *Proceedings of the Philosophy of Education Society of Great Britain*, vol. VI, no. 2, July 1972.

The nature of historical knowledge is discussed in P. Gardiner, *The Nature of Historical Explanation*, Oxford University Press, 1968; P. Gardiner, 'Historical Understanding and the Empiricist Tradition', in B. Williams and A. Montefiore (eds), *British Analytical Philosophy*, Routledge & Kegan Paul, 1966; and W. H. Dray, *Philosophy of History*, Prentice-Hall, 1964.

Bibliography

AYER, A. J. (1936), *Language, Truth and Logic*, Gollancz (Penguin, 1971).
BERLIN, I. (1972), 'Giambattista Vico', *Listener*, 28 September.
CASSIRER, E. (1944), *An Essay on Man*, Yale University Press.
DEARDEN, R. F. (1968), *The Philosophy of Primary Education*, Routledge & Kegan Paul.

GARDINER, P. (1968), *The Nature of Historical Explanation,* Oxford University Press.

GRIFFITHS, P. (1957), 'The justification of the principle of rational benevolence', *Proceedings of the Aristotelian Society.*

HINDESS, E. (1972), 'Forms of knowledge', in *Proceedings of the Philosophy of Education Society of Great Britain,* vol. VI, no. 2, July.

HIRST, P. H. (1969), 'The logic of the curriculum', *Journal of Curriculum Studies,* vol. I, no. 2.

HIRST, P. H. and PETERS, R. S. (1970), *The Logic of Education,* Routledge & Kegan Paul.

OAKESHOTT, M. (1962), 'The Voice of Poetry in the Conversation of Mankind' in *Rationalism in Politics,* Methuen.

PHENIX, P. H. (1964), *Realms of Meaning,* McGraw-Hill.

ROWSE, A. et al. (1973), 'The teaching of history', *Times Educational Supplement,* 23 March.

WINCH, P. (1958), *The Idea of a Social Science and its Relation to Philosophy,* Routledge & Kegan Paul.

Chapter seven

The curriculum

D.S. Wringe

I said at the end of chapter 6 that if Hirst's account of the curriculum is correct, and that if there are in fact a number of distinct forms of knowledge, then this ought to be of practical help to those people who have the job of actually sitting down and planning the curriculum, be it the class teacher herself in the infant school or a committee of heads of department in a large secondary school.

But, I also added that there is disagreement about how far this account *is* actually helpful in this way.

It may already have occurred to you that there is something apparently very old-fashioned in all this talk about true statements in terms of which the forms of knowledge have been characterised. Surely these days we ought to regard with scorn approaches to education which make the learning of facts central, and look rather with favour on notions like 'problem-solving', 'self-expression', 'creative activity' and the like.

Second, you may have thought that it is very odd to be giving a careful characterisation of the logically distinct forms of knowledge at a time when there is so much talk in other quarters about the need to break down subject barriers, to use topic-based or interdisciplinary approaches – in short to work for integration in education.

Third, you may have wondered why we should pay very much attention to this kind of account at all, since if we decide *what* to teach pupils from the point of view of the nature and structure of knowledge (instead of the nature and structure of the child) we may seem to be putting the cart before the horse.

In other words you may ask 'Wouldn't it be altogether more sensible to find out what children are capable of and interested in learning before deciding by reference to a rather abstract model of knowledge what we are going to teach them?'

These three reservations are, I think, justified. What is needed, then, is an attempt to show how a philosophical view about the nature and structure of knowledge *can* shed light on curriculum planning without necessarily being a rearguard action to defend the *status quo*.

The rest of this chapter will therefore be devoted to looking at the three possible ways in which curriculum planners might object to the forms of knowledge account and to showing how these objections might be faced and overcome.

Facts and the curriculum

The first objection to approaching curriculum planning by considering what forms of knowledge there are is that we may be tempted to place too great an emphasis on the place of facts in education (Warnock, 1971). After all the forms of knowledge were characterised by examining the different kinds of statement which it is possible to call true and to defend as true in a variety of ways. So mastery of such forms might reasonably be thought to be mastery of a variety of true statements. On this view then education would indeed appear to be a very 'intellectual' business. This is because a person would be held to be more or less educated according to the progress he had made in understanding a number of true statements within the various forms.

But many people would think that to regard educational achievements as purely 'cognitive' in this sense is an extremely retrograde step. They would probably argue this on two grounds. First they would claim that this is a very limited way of characterising knowledge and its significance in human life. Second, they would say that if knowledge *is* to be characterised in this way many pupils will be unable to make very much educational progress. This second point will be taken up again in the third section of this chapter. Let us for a moment examine the first argument — namely that the belief that there are distinct forms of knowledge *necessarily* implies a very intellectual approach to education.

Those who make this kind of objection are often concerned to point out that, as well as wanting children to learn a great number of facts, they also hope that they will learn to perform a great range of skills. They want children to read and write, to learn to swim and play games, to play musical instruments, make mathematical calculations, scientific experiments and so on. Others would point to the importance in children's education of the range and quality of emotional experiences which they are given and which otherwise would be impossible for them. Bantock (1971, p. 260), for example, writing on the curriculum has said

Furthermore the emphasis on the *affective* . . . points to the need for an education of the emotions in ways which our cognitive curriculum sorely neglects. Freud has shown the extent to which our emotional life is fundamental and the arts provide the traditional means by which we can seek to come to terms with these emotions.

These different emphases among educationists are interesting because they can be seen as reflecting different *philosophical* views about the nature of knowledge.

Thus for example someone like Ryle would tend to argue that our knowledge *is* our ability to perform in this or that way rather than any set of true beliefs which we may have. On the other hand someone like Polanyi whose views are quoted by Reid would say that our knowledge includes a kind of inner experience which is *different* from whatever true statements we may be able to make. He would say, for example, that when we recognise a face this depends on our 'knowing' a great deal more than we could actually set out in a list of statements.

So there is some philosophical controversy about how to characterise the knowledge a person has. This being so, it is possible perhaps to understand why Richmond in his book on the curriculum (1971, p. 200) criticises Hirst for failing to allow that sometimes our knowledge *comes out* in what we do and sometimes in what we experience or perceive as well as in what we believe; and that these are all important aspects of our knowledge.

Now if you are yourself inclined to think that when we teach pupils we are concerned to teach them not only *that* certain things are true but also to be able to perform certain skills, and to be capable of certain emotional and perceptual experiences, then you will want to know whether, in fact, it is possible to reconcile your convictions with Hirst's view that we should characterise knowledge in terms of a number of forms.

The answer to this is surely 'yes'. After all it is possible to hold that facts are important in education without holding that only facts are important. But more than this, it is possible to argue that there is a very tight connection between what we know in a factual sense and our ability to feel certain things or to perform in certain ways even if these are different achievements.

To take an example from moral education, we cannot feel guilty for example unless we know what we have done wrong, what 'wrong' means and so on. Similarly we cannot attempt to put things right unless we know what would count as putting them right. Again we might argue in the area of aesthetics that we cannot experience the enjoyment of a film or play or picture if we do not know what it is about, nor can we learn to perform effectively in the arts, whether it be to produce an effective collage or soap carving or a piece of mime or film, without knowing what counts as performing successfully in any of these ways.

All this is to make a logical point. It is to show that the things we know, do and feel are interrelated. Indeed Bantock himself stresses this point when he says: 'It is a fundamental error not to see that as the arts develop they inevitably come to involve knowledge and understanding' (1971, p. 263), although he makes this remark in a context where he is stressing the importance of trying to develop bodily awareness through various kinds of activity including drama and movement.

But we must be careful. We do not have to argue that because knowing, doing and feeling are interrelated that we should always try to get people to learn to *do* things, for example to speak a foreign language, by telling them truths about it. On the other hand it does not follow either that we should *never* try to improve somebody's ability to perform or to change somebody's perception of a situation by telling him things. So even if we are now agreed that in education we are concerned with people's ability to perform in certain ways, to extend the range of their emotional experience as well as the range of their understanding, a great deal still has to be settled about the best way of doing all this.

But perhaps you can now see why it is possible to hold that understanding is central in education without necessarily underestimating the importance of doing or feeling. It is just that what we do and feel is inextricably linked up with what we know. So it is quite possible to find Hirst's characterisation of knowledge helpful when planning a curriculum. This is because we are not bound to infer from it either a fact-laden curriculum, nor even a particularly didactic approach to teaching.

Integration and the curriculum

The second objection to finding any educational significance in the forms of knowledge account is that it seems to be out of all keeping with attempts to break down subject-centred approaches to the time-table, to adopt project or topic methods or to try various ways of interrelating what is taught to pupils. In short it seems opposed to all attempts to work for integration in education.

In assessing the strength of this objection we must consider the following questions. Does the belief that there are various forms of knowledge inevitably commit us to a view that a subject-centred time-table is most appropriate? Does it necessarily involve us in abandoning project- or topic-based methods? If furthermore we think that integration is an important concept why do we think this?

Let us consider these questions in turn. First, then, if we believe that there are distinct forms of knowledge does it necessarily follow that we ought to adopt a subject-centred timetable? I suppose that somebody might argue that the timetable should actually be a mirror reflection, as it were, of the forms of knowledge. If he did think this then he would still have to say why. After all, if we take the forms as being something rather like science, mathematics, interpersonal knowledge and so on and we take a traditional junior school or secondary school timetable, the latter do not *in fact* look like a reflection of the former. We have to resort to Hirst's concept of a field of knowledge to explain the status of some of the areas.

On Hirst's account (in 'Liberal Education and the Nature of Knowledge') a field of knowledge represents an area in which subject-matter is brought together from different forms of knowledge according to some particular criterion of relevance. To take his own example, if we are interested in the study of man in relation to his environment then there is a body of knowledge relevant to this study, namely geography. This body of knowledge does not *itself* constitute a particular form (as defined) but it may nevertheless draw upon several of the forms.

Another important example of a field of knowledge is in the area where important practical decisions have to be made. If one is deciding where it would be best to build a new airport, for example, knowledge drawn from a number of forms of knowledge may well contribute to the final decision.

Now given these two concepts of *forms* of knowledge and *fields* of knowledge it is possible to make out two extreme cases in respect of the curriculum. As we have seen one way of arguing would be to say that we should start afresh and bring all curricula into line with what the forms of knowledge actually are. Alternatively it might be claimed that we should construct the curriculum solely in terms of whatever 'fields' of knowledge (or topics or themes) we take to be particularly relevant for our pupils.

Now the first move would have certain advantages. After all, if the development of mind is inextricably linked with our initiation into the forms of knowledge then we should, on the face of it at least, be setting about things in the way most likely to develop people's minds. But even if somebody did try to argue that the curriculum ought to reflect the forms of knowledge just like that, there remain at least three important problems which would show that this approach to curriculum planning is oversimplified, to say the least.

First, even if we were clear just what the forms of knowledge were, we should still be left with an enormous amount of work to do in deciding what to put on the curriculum to represent each particular form, given the enormous amount of knowledge which each form embraces. I have already indicated in chapter 6 how, for example, the natural sciences may be said to include geology, physics, chemistry, biology, biochemistry and so on.

Second, it may not be possible or even desirable to represent some of the forms of knowledge explicitly on the timetable just like that. Possibly a great deal of moral awareness can be developed in pupils if

teachers exploit informally situations in schools in which moral problems actually arise. Again the best way to achieve interpersonal understanding may be by keeping on the timetable those 'traditional' subjects
such as literature and history, the study of which necessarily contribute
to the understanding of other minds.

Third, it would in fact be to misrepresent Hirst to suggest that the
various forms of knowledge, though logically distinct in the ways specified, are not, nevertheless, inte-related in important ways. Thus he
argues that to understand some of the physical sciences it is first necessary to know a great deal of mathematics. Also one might claim that a
great deal of factual knowledge about how people really think and act
is necessary before one can appreciate literary works of art.

From this it can be seen that the belief that we ought to plan the
curriculum in the light of our understanding of the forms of knowledge
could be rather naïve. Such a belief needs careful and detailed working
out, even in terms of what can be inferred from the forms of knowledge
account itself, if it is to be at all sound.

The alternative move is to argue that a curriculum which aims to
mirror the forms of knowledge may well seem extremely arbitrary to
the pupils. And if you think that the curriculum ought to be planned in
such a way that what we teach pupils should be brought together under
headings which make sense to *them,* then you may well favour
approaching the curriculum in terms of 'fields' rather than 'forms' or,
to use the current jargon, in terms of 'topics' or 'themes'.

It is at this point in fact that pleas for integration are usually made.
For the themes or topics chosen for study in integrated approaches are
frequently picked because they are held to be relevant to pupils, whereas a study of the forms of knowledge in themselves is held to be
irrelevant and boring. So it is at this point that we must ask whether it
is desirable to plan the curriculum in terms of fields rather than forms.
Before attempting to settle this question however, let us first consider
the notion of 'integration' itself.

It will be enough to indicate some of the contemporary confusion
over the meaning of the term 'integration' by referring to a copy of an
educational journal which is itself an attempt to show integration at
work. It consists of articles as diverse as the following, but all on the
theme of integration: integrated studies, the integrated community, the
integrated day, the integrated personality.

From this example we can see how essential it is to get clear what
might be meant by integration when applied to the curriculum. D. I.
Lloyd, in his article on the integrated day (1971, p. 20), suggests that

to integrate means to make up a whole from separate parts, to
combine separate elements. The implication behind a desire to
integrate therefore is that the parts lack something. So before we are

justified in using the word in any context we must establish whether what is before us are really parts at all.

Now it will be already clear from the account given of the forms of knowledge that we can hardly view knowledge itself as forming a whole in this sense, or even a person's understanding. Rather it would seem that the greater a person's understanding, the more differentiated his consciousness is because he has been initiated into several extremely different modes of understanding.

Nevertheless it is true, as has been already stated, that at least one important kind of knowledge, namely the ability to make certain kinds of practical judgment *does* require the ability to bring together relevant considerations from different forms of knowledge, and this fact certainly ought to be considered when planning the curriculum. Thus, no doubt, part of the curriculum in the latter years of the secondary school ought to be devoted to a study of problems requiring the exercise of practical judgment. This intention clearly lies behind the work of the Schools' Council Humanities Project and their attempt to provide materials from a number of disciplines which would help children to make informed judgments on matters likely to arise in the course of their daily lives, such as the role of the family today, problems of race relations and so on.

But let us now return to my original question whether we should plan the entire curriculum at either junior or secondary level in terms of themes or topics. Obviously the answer to this depends in part on the extent to which the coverage of these is compatible with initiating pupils into the different forms of knowledge. However the reason often given for choosing broad areas of study is that these are held to take into account what pupils find relevant or are currently interested in.

Thus, if we take the example of an account of a European Studies course for secondary pupils of all abilities which includes some study of the cultural, social, economic and political conditions of some of the EEC countries we find that it is defended partly at least on the grounds that such studies simply are relevant for future citizens of the European community (Jones, 1972).

Now this kind of appeal to what is relevant to pupils is clearly persuasive. Nevertheless there are certain difficulties in adopting this kind of justification when planning the curriculum. It is after all always open to question whether what has been chosen as suitable for integrated approaches does in fact seem as important and fascinating to pupils as is claimed. Indeed we might say that the conditions under which pupils come to see knowledge as relevant, and what is taught as interesting is much more complex than the thinking behind many integrated approaches seems to imply. Thus it may well be soundest in the long run to decide first what pupils ought to know, or ought to find relevant and then to concentrate resources on finding ways of making it seem so. This can be settled however independently of the question whether the curriculum should be 'integrated' or not.

In other words if you now agree that we are really concerned with what it is in the pupil's best interest to know when planning the curriculum then it is possible to argue that *all* pupils should have some grounding in each of the forms of knowledge, if this is taken to be inextricably linked with the development of mind. On the other hand it is by no means clear that this general objective — namely the initiation of pupils into the different forms of knowledge — cannot be achieved by planning a curriculum which consists in part of certain forms of knowledge such as mathematics and in part of themes or topics, provided these are treated in a way which leads to a properly differentiated understanding.

Not everybody, however, would agree that we should have the same general objectives for all pupils and for this reason I shall now go on in the next section to consider whether this is in fact desirable.

The common curriculum

I said in the introduction to this chapter that the third objection which people might make to basing the curriculum on the forms of knowledge is that it seems to be setting about things in the wrong order. This is because some people might argue that we ought to plan the curriculum in the light of what we know about the child, namely his age, intellectual stage of development, general ability and social background, his own interests, special needs and so on.

Now it could be argued that to plan what would effectively be very different curricula for separate individuals could lead to certain children being seriously educationally deprived. Others would say on the contrary that it is *only* by providing very different curricula, possibly even in different schools, that we are really providing equality of opportunity at all.

Hirst's position on this is very clear: 'If the acquisition of certain fundamental elements of knowledge is necessary for the achievement of the rational mind in some particular respect then these at any rate cannot but be universal objectives for the curriculum' (Hirst, 1969, p. 153).

His argument has been extended by J. P. White along the lines that follow. He argues that we can identify a 'higher culture' into which every secondary child should be initiated. He specifies as components of this culture activities like the arts, mathematics, the human and physical sciences and philosophy. That is, he picks out 'those activities whose nature, unlike cookery say or cricket, is utterly incomprehensible until one begins to engage in them'. He goes so far as to state 'None shall be allowed to drop any of these disciplines until he is sufficiently on the inside of it to understand why its devotees are devoted to it' (White, 1969, p. 275). This would mean in practice that every child should carry all these disciplines to something like sixth-form level.

Of course he faces the problem on this argument that we should often be in a position of compelling people to study subjects they did not want to do. For him the way out of the dilemma is to try to devise methods of getting people to study the appropriate disciplines in ways they do find agreeable. He argues that because a subject is compulsory we need not coerce people to study it and this view links up with the conclusion reached towards the end of the section of this chapter on integration and the curriculum.

Not surprisingly, however, this view of what the curriculum should contain has met with considerable opposition on a number of grounds. In the first place it explicitly suggests that there is a 'higher' culture. There is, therefore, presumably a 'lower' culture into which many pupils would normally be initiated unless steps were taken in schools to wean them away from it. Now you might feel like saying that the curriculum should reflect the culture which is that of the children who attend the school and of their parents. You might argue this on the grounds that the proper way of seeing the situation is as one in which there are simply 'different' cultures, not higher or lower ones. Then again you might want to raise questions about the possible effects of alienating children from their own culture by introducing them to a significantly different one. Finally you might want to argue that, simply on practical grounds, the more the curriculum is based on the culture which is typical of the community within which the school exists the more chance there is of making effective educational contact with pupils in the schools.

But all these arguments have to be set against the view that to make progress within the forms of knowledge is to develop one's mind in a way which makes possible a freedom of choice in one's life which no other education could achieve.

Some people object to the common curriculum on different grounds. For them it is not a matter of whether one should presume to impose a middle-class culture on non-middle-class children. They are simply aware that some children are less well equipped to deal with a very linguistically biased curriculum. They may think in any case that verbal achievements are not the only valid form of academic achievement. Thus, for both these reasons they would advocate markedly different curricula for children with different kinds of linguistic competence, and would regard this as one way of implementing the principle of equality in education.

So Bantock, whose ideas on the curriculum I discussed earlier would

argue for a curriculum in which 'for children whose minds find existence easier to grasp in terms of the concrete and particular and who
need help in coping with cultural media which are the prime influences
in their lives to an extent which the book is not' (Bantock, 1971, p.
263), three-fifths of the time should be taken up with practical activities like the arts and games, outward-bound projects and so on.

The reply to this kind of argument is twofold. On the one hand we
cannot logically infer any particular curriculum from the simple fact
that some children are linguistically disadvantaged unless we also hold
that it is *impossible* for them to make progress within a linguistically
biased curriculum. At the moment, it seems, this would be a view based
merely on prejudice.

Second, if those practical activities which are held to be valuable
for the less able really *are* the valid educational enterprise it is claimed,
then these too should be offered to those of average and above average
ability as well.

The problem then is one of safeguarding for all pupils the kind of
curriculum which, it is argued, is intimately connected with the
development of mind while at the same time insisting that this is *not*
simply a cognitive or intellectual business, as I tried to point out in the
first section. Equally we must recognise that pupils are very differently
equipped (for all sorts of reasons to do with their motivation, their
ability and so on) to make progress within the forms of knowledge.
This means that the greatest flexibility is needed in planning approaches
which meet pupils on their own terms and truly start from where they
are. But this flexibility of approach should always be seen for what it is
— namely an attempt to make some initiation into the forms of knowledge a real possibility for all pupils.

Conclusion

I tried in chapter 6 to explain what is meant both by the claim that
there are various forms of knowledge and by the claim that this fact is
of the utmost significance in human life.

In this chapter I have tried to show how far and in what ways this
view of knowledge is compelling when we set about planning the curriculum. In the first section I attempted to show that certain objections
to describing knowledge in this way are invalid. I tried in the second
section to show the limits to what can be *directly* inferred from this
view of knowledge and, finally, I have indicated what conclusions seem
to me to be inescapable for curriculum planning if this view of knowledge is accepted as correct.

D. S. Wringe

Further reading

For a general discussion of knowledge and the curriculum, readers are referred to P. H. Hirst and R. S. Peters, *The Logic of Education,* Routledge & Kegan Paul, 1970. Two contrasting philosophical views of the nature of knowledge may be found in G. Ryle, *The Concept of Mind,* 1949 (edition used, Penguin, 1963); and L. A. Reid, 'The arts, knowledge and education', *British Journal of Educational Studies,* June 1967. A central account of the forms of knowledge and their significance for education is to be found in P. H. Hirst, 'Liberal Education and the Nature of Knowledge', in R. D. Archambault (ed.), *Philosophical Analysis and Education,* Routledge & Kegan Paul, 1965. A collection of papers in R. Hooper (ed.), *The Curriculum: Context, Design and Development,* Oliver & Boyd, 1971, contains important contributions relating to the curriculum. The theme of curriculum integration is dealt with in R. Pring, 'Curriculum integration', *University of London Institute of Education Bulletin,* Spring Term, 1970; and J. P. White, *Towards a Compulsory Curriculum,* Routledge & Kegan Paul, 1973, contains a detailed defence of the compulsory curriculum.

Bibliography

BANTOCK, G. (1971), 'Towards a theory of popular education', *Times Educational Supplement,* 12 March 1971, 19 March 1971, reprinted in Hooper, R. (ed.), *The Curriculum: Context, Design and Development,* Oliver & Boyd.
HIRST, P. H. (1969), 'The logic of the curriculum', *Journal of Curriculum Studies,* vol. I, no. 2.
JONES, B. (1972), 'European studies', *New Era,* vol. 53, no. 10, December.
LLOYD, D. I. (1971), 'The Integrated Day in the Primary School', in Walton, J. (ed.), *The Integrated Day in Theory and Practice,* Ward Lock Educational.
RICHMOND, W. K. (1971), *The School Curriculum,* Methuen.
WARNOCK, M. (1971), 'Giving facts a good name', *New Society,* 17 June.
WHITE, J. P. (1969), 'The curriculum mongers: education in reverse', *New Society,* 6 March, reprinted in Hooper, R. (ed.), *The Curriculum: Context, Design and Development,* Oliver & Boyd, 1971.

Chapter eight

Traditional and progressive education

D.I. Lloyd

The newcomer to education soon finds that here, as in religion and politics, there are opposing sides. But instead of fundamentalist *v.* liberal, or Conservative *v.* Labour, he finds traditionalist *v.* progressive. Before long he feels he has to show his allegiance to one rather than the other, and it is at this point that the danger arises. For, as in many other aspects of life, instead of choosing freely, from both, those beliefs and attitudes which he considers good and proper, he finds he is expected to make a choice of one side or the other. He cannot select what he wants. This results in members of opposite camps having extreme views of each other, just as happens in racial conflicts, and showing a tendency to be uncritical of their side and excessively critical of the other.

If, then, you are a traditionalist, it may be assumed you are a stick-in-the-mud, past forty, a Black Paper sympathiser and obsessed with standards. If you are a progressive, you are keen, have youth on your side and seize on anything new that dawns on the horizon of the Teacher's centre. In fact, we might make a list of such popular distinctions. Here is a sample.

Traditionalist	*Progressive*
teaches subjects	teaches children
uses logic	uses intuition
teaches the intellect	educates the emotions
is keen on standards	considers happiness more important
regards teaching as tedious	thinks teaching is fun
uses class lessons only	employs individual or group methods
is boss	is a friend
produces a repressive atmosphere	creates free and easy climate
uses rote methods	ensures learning is by doing

D. I. Lloyd

Of course, whether you accept any of the features listed as true or not will depend partly on which side you are on. Each of these descriptions may be true, partially true or false. What must be resisted is the wholesale acceptance of them as accurate descriptions of any teacher merely because one or two of the items happen to be true.

John Dewey the American educationist (1963, ch. 1) was very much aware of the danger of over-simplified classification. Opposing sides often create stereotypes or caricatures of each other because it makes them feel more secure. Here, the traditionalist becomes for the progressive someone with a stick beating the children into submitting to knowledge and the progressive for the traditionalist, someone whom you cannot see for children, and who is so concerned for their happiness that he does not bother about what, if anything, is being learned.

Another weapon in the battle of derision between the two sides is the use of slogans or expressions like: 'Children do not know what is good for them', 'No real learning ever takes place unless they like what they learn', 'Children like organisation' and 'How they learn is far more important than what they learn'. These statements, amongst many others, are used to support all manner of different teaching methods, so that any such statement on its own is of little help in telling us what the speaker's views are. For example, children do like organisation — of a kind, but which kind? The headmaster who told two students that he ran his school like an army regiment and that they were to adopt similar methods on school practice believed in organisation; as does the infant teacher who arrives before school in order to put out different activities for her reception class. It is then not helpful to justify what one is doing by resort to statements which can be used by opposing sides. Both the parson and the playboy can say 'I'm all for getting the best out of life'. What, of course, they actually get out of it is quite different and can only be assessed by seeing how they lead their lives. So, too, with these two kinds of teacher.

The sad consequence of this opposition in education is that 'informal' teachers, using, say, an integrated day approach, feel guilty if they take a class lesson, and 'formal' teachers that they are capitulating to the opposition if they sometimes adopt group methods. The self-defence that is used in the face of a challenge that older teachers should have tried other ways of teaching, takes the form 'When you have been teaching as long as I have . . .', whilst younger teachers not too ready to learn from their elders often speak as if there had been no good teaching before the last war.

The differences, then, between teachers over matters in education are often emotional rather than rational. It is regrettable that such a state of affairs exists, for this inhibits teachers from selecting from a wide range of methods those most suitable to their personality and preference. We need to look more closely at both traditional and progressive education for, though there are some real differences between them, there is more variety in each than we are often aware of or care to admit. This will help us to see more value in each and to select what we feel is best from each.

Traditional education

Traditional education offers two main approaches. At one time they were found in private and state education respectively. For the education of the well-to-do, there was an emphasis on the classical subjects. These subjects were taught not merely for their bearing on real life, but also, perhaps mainly, as valuable in their own right. Side by side with those subjects of the 'intellect' was physical training which ensured that the mind was in a sound body.

The other approach is more recent and is found in the state schools which grew rapidly in number in the last century. Its aims were to make children literate and moral and to enable them to earn a living and find a useful place in society. The most remarkable kind of school during that period was the monitorial school which sometimes taught as many as a thousand children in one hall. This school system was highly efficient, at least in its own terms, and was based on the factory system.

With the introduction of Robert Lowe's Revised Code, 1862, the curriculum in the state schools consisted solely of the three Rs, reading, writing and arithmetic. Teachers' salaries were directly related to the successes of their pupils in examinations in these subjects. This put undue pressure on them and on their pupils who were subjected to all manner of measures taken to ensure that the level of salaries was maintained. Teachers often had to ignore the less able children who were unlikely to pass the examinations. Their teaching methods encouraged rote learning and were supported by punishment of which corporal punishment was a common form. Gradually, the curriculum came to include other subjects but then only for the older children, for there was a strong feeling that children should not learn more than was needed for their position in society.

These two main approaches in traditional education, with their different curricula, were justified on quite different grounds — one intrinsic and the other utilitarian. What was common to both was their view of education as something that had to be 'put into' children. The language they employed showed this. The teacher was said to 'inculcate good taste', 'to imbue with the love of learning', 'to infuse ideas', 'to instil wisdom', 'to implant good sense' and, more colloquially, 'to ensure that something sinks in'. Here, then, the teacher was the one who was in possession of knowledge and the child the ignorant and largely unthinking being to whom this knowledge must be passed on.

91

The child had few features of his own. The emphasis was on what he was to become rather than what he was. And for some, the nature of the child was such that even when he was being taught what was good he would show resistance to it — the doctrine of original sin. That he did not like school was evidence of that. The possibility that his dislike was a reflection on the inadequacy of the teaching methods was not considered (a good example of a self-fulfilling prophecy). If he did not learn then it was because he was stupid. We have come a long way since then and take for granted our understanding of a vast range of individual differences and the study of child development, which at that time did not exist.

Comment

What can we say for and against these forms of education? First, the form which stressed that education is valuable in its own right finds strong support today (Peters, 1965). Expressions such as 'ways of life', 'dimensions of understanding', 'forms of knowledge' and 'modes of experience' have been used to describe what is regarded as valuable in human experience. This is a very important justification for education but I shall say no more on this topic as it has been treated fully in chapter 6.

The other form, the utilitarian, had a great deal of practical success. In a short time, vast numbers of children became literate, so changing a situation which had existed for centuries. Again, school children during the First World War, for example, contributed to the war effort by making crutches, bedrests and sandbags and spent more time than they would have normally in cultivating what had been their playing fields. Whether there was too much concentration on the utilitarian aspect and whether that aspect itself was morally justifiable is to be questioned. The general point is that some recognition has been given to non-educational interests in schooling.

What were its failings? State education, which was largely utilitarian, had a limited view of the nature of education. Its education was mechanical in character and children were given little to raise their quality of life. Its curriculum was narrow. Its view of the child's mind as a mere receptacle for knowledge or as something corrupted by original sin, has frequently been challenged. The methods employed were largely verbal and the child was not physically active in his learning. Few experiences were first hand — a fact which, it could be argued, severely limited the understanding. Its punitive methods tended to alienate a child from education rather than encourage respect for it. But it would be wrong to think that all teachers were sadists. Doctors at one time used leeches to effect a cure. They were mistaken and may have caused unnecessary pain but it cannot be denied that they had the interests of their patients at heart. So, too, whilst many of the methods the traditional teacher employed may have had questionable value, it would be a mistake to think that those bad methods implied bad motives. A particularly striking example of this point is in D. Salmon (1914). 'The whole routine', he writes, 'should be regulated literally by clockwork.' In a footnote he is so conscious of time-wasting that he calculates 'if a class of thirty children spends a minute more than is necessary in changing lessons, for instance, half an hour is wasted'. It would be easy to label such a person an authoritarian who controlled his class in a rigid way, ignoring the individual differences of his pupils. Yet, a little earlier in the book, he advises teachers to take account of their pupils' natures and reminds us of the attitudes we should adopt in our relationships with them.

> The man or woman who does not feel deep and abiding love for children, who does not watch with interest the unfolding of their minds, who is not ready to share in their games as well as their tasks, who does not sympathise with the most troublesome, who does not recognise the infinite possibilities of their natures, has no right to be a teacher.

Here again we have an instance of teaching where we could have criticised a form of teaching too readily, without finding out enough about the motives behind it; and so showed the same kind of insensitivity towards the teachers who used it that we would have charged them with towards their pupils.

The caution recommended at the beginning of this chapter and supported by the above example is something that needs to be remembered when we judge our colleagues. Many teachers, for example, place themselves in the 'traditional' class. Whilst this gives an indication of their educational position, it is a very vague one. We need to know more. A person's view of teaching cannot be assessed until certain questions have been asked, such as 'Do you think some subjects are more important than others?', 'To what extent do you use punishment in your teaching?', 'How far is first hand experience necessary and possible in the time available?', 'How far is it advisable to use group and individual, as well as class, methods?' Only then are we in a position to comment on his teaching. My guess is that we would be surprised at the variety of answers we would get from teachers who claim to be traditionalists.

Progressive education

First, an observation on the word 'progressive'. It does not imply just change, but development – that is, change for the better. It is wrong, therefore, to call any innovation progressive. Closer examination may show it to be a change for the worse. Advertisements constantly impress on us the newness of certain products, implying that they are an improvement on earlier ones. A little reflection will convince us that this is frequently false.

What then of progressive education? In England, it began in a small number of boarding schools. The first of these was established by Cecil Reddie at Abbotsholme in 1889. Other schools were formed soon after and by 1934 there were twenty-one such schools. The movement had no clear ideology. R. J. W. Selleck in his interesting book on this subject, *English Primary Education and the Progressives, 1914–1939* (1972), writes (pp. 62–3):

> The progressives were not a disciplined army marching, united, on a particular town. They were a group of travellers who, finding themselves together on the road, had formed a loosely united band. They did not all intend to finish in the same town and while on the journey some were to leave the band and new travellers were to join it. . . . Observers who watched them from a distance sometimes thought they were pilgrims.

Amongst them, for example, were Christians, Theosophists, orientalists and atheists. Edmond Holmes, the Board's Chief Inspector, was influenced by oriental religion whilst Maria Montessori was a staunch Catholic. They often disagreed amongst themselves. Montessori had been criticised by A. S. Neill of Summerhill. Another said she knew little of children. Their thinking was influenced by different people. The thinking of Freud was incorporated into the educational ideas of some. Others looked further back to Herbart and Froebel. Some relied more on orthodox psychology. Yet even with these differences and disagreements, they had some views in common. Many of them came together at a conference in 1915, entitled 'New Ideals in Education', to discuss their views. From Edward Blishen (1969) and R. Skidelsky (1969) we can summarise some of them.

1   The schools were usually boarding. Few were single-sex, many were co-educational.

2   Though they emphasised the spiritual side of human nature, they did not align themselves to any particular church body, because most rejected the belief in the inherited sin of man.

3   Their curriculum reflected a shift away from the classical tradition and they included some of the following in their syllabuses; music, art, history, crafts as well as activities involving manual labour.

4   The emotional side of man was seen to be good; and in learning, as important as, if not more important than, intelligence. Here developmental psychology, the study of individual difference, which has its roots in Rousseau, received much attention.

5   This was all part of a larger view which was that the child should be considered in all aspects of his nature, physical, social, emotional and intellectual.

6   Learning should involve direct experience. Book learning was secondhand and so it could not involve the whole personality of the child.

7   Their attitude towards misdemeanours and punishment differed markedly from that of the traditionalists. There was no physical punishment, and where punishment did exist it took the form of deprivation of privilege. The lack of emphasis on punishment resulted from the belief that the misbehaviour of the child had been brought about by causes beyond his control, and was, therefore, unintentional.

8   The teacher was not seen as one who had the sole right to make decisions for everyone in school but the children, too, were regarded as having the right to take part in the running of the school. The belief that the teacher alone knew what was good for his pupils was regarded as false. In more modern terms, progressives wanted children to participate in the authority structure of the school.

In chapters 4 and 5 of his book Selleck shows how in time progressive thinking affected state education in its curriculum and methods of teaching. The *Handbook of Suggestions for Teachers* moved steadily towards progressive ideas between its 1905 edition and that of 1937. There was now considerable emphasis on the individual, the keystone of the movement. In the 1937 edition the difference in curriculum content is clear. 'English' had become 'English Language and Literature' with explicit advice that grammar should be taught less formally and that reading was to include literature and not just mechanical word recognition. Mathematics replaced arithmetic and there was to be less stress on speed and accuracy and more on understanding. In other subjects, too, there were suggestions that the content of the curriculum should be changed. In the Hadow Report (1931), there is ample evidence of the influence of progressive thinking. Their stress on co-operation rather than competition now appeared in an official report: 'A good school, in short, is not a place of compulsory instruction, but a community of old and young, engaged in learning by co-operative experiment.' This report Selleck claims, popularised progressive education and made it respectable. A glance at the paragraph headings of the Plowden Report shows that it has continued this trend. Progressive thinking is without doubt very much part of the fabric of our present-day education. Almost all junior schools and many secondary schools and colleges are co-educational; our curriculum is broader; views on punishment, especially corporal punishment, have changed and participation in school government, not an uncommon phenomenon. These are historical facts. We must ask now, are they changes for the better?

D. I. Lloyd

Comment

The extension of the curriculum by adding music, history, and art was something to be welcomed, though their introduction was not quite for the reasons outlined in chapter 5. The belief here is that man is more than intellect; that emotion is an important part of human nature and has a right to expression. What is not clear is the justification that the progressives give for their viewpoint.

We said that the keystone of the movement was its concern with the pupil as an individual. The whole atmosphere within which the relationship between teacher and pupil operated was such that respect for the pupil could not have been greater. There existed a strong desire to make him happy, to keep him interested, to understand him at each stage of his development; in a word, to view him as a person in his own right. This is in sharp contrast with the other view in which childhood was seen as merely a means to an end, adulthood, and possibly membership of society. If we read virtually any biography of the last century, we come across the belief that children should be seen and not heard. This does not indicate that there is less cruelty to children today than there was in those days, but rather that the attitude of adults to children has changed; and the fact that a large section of society is now looked at differently represents a considerable change in our moral outlook. From this increased respect for children has sprung the vast amount of literature and research that has grown up on the development of children. We now have studies of children ranging from their seemingly random movements before birth to the kind of friendships that they form in a secondary school. The one is a study of physical development, the other, using sociometric techniques, a study in social psychology. All such studies have the aim of finding out more about the child so that we may know how to treat him properly.

Can there be anything questionable about what seem to be very moral and high-minded beliefs? Unfortunately, there is. So often in education, as I suppose elsewhere, when something that is good is regarded as the only good it brings discredit on itself. In progressive education, with its emphasis largely on the child and his development, under the influence of the idea of the child as an organism, not enough attention has been given to the goal of that organism's growth. The danger with any analogy, such as that between a child's development and the stages of a plant's growth, is that it can be taken too far. The plant has its final form from the start in embryonic form. This is not so with children. It is precisely the purpose of education to develop in the child those attitudes and beliefs he would not have acquired otherwise. At birth the child is no more than a physical organism, a non-moral being, without any attitudes, beliefs or knowledge. These he will begin to acquire fairly quickly. So whilst on the one hand we must in no way undervalue the importance of the progressive emphasis on development, the direction of that development cannot be inferred from the nature of the child. Whilst the job of the teacher is to be aware of the nature of the child, he brings to it, as does the artist to his material, a quality which it does not possess in its natural state. He does this whether he is aware of it or not. This explains why the progressives, in spite of thinking they were not changing the natural inclinations of the child, often planned different curricula and usually taught with different methods. The disagreements they had with one another were really not so much about the nature of the child but about the nature of education.

Difficulties also are in the attitude of the progressive towards authority. The traditionalist lays stress on the teacher and his knowledge whilst the progressive emphasises the child's freedom to choose. How this choice can be free is difficult to see, for education is not just concerned with allowing people to choose, but, more fundamentally, with enabling them to see what choices are available. The first step to choosing between painting a ship and writing a simple poem, or choosing between Latin and German, is to be educated into seeing that there are these choices and what they mean. If a child cannot understand what he is choosing, he is not really choosing but engaged in a school-like lucky-dip. Freedom presupposes understanding, of which the teacher is the medium. Without understanding, freedom in some progressive schools, as Dewey pointed out, would become licence (Dewey, 1963).

Many progressive teachers claim that they are influencing the child very little, but this is not a true picture of what they are doing. They may believe that the child really is being his true self, with themselves staying on the touchline, merely giving support. Yet when we plan our class, arrange our room, organise our time, purchase our materials, we must have some idea of what we want the children to achieve. Furthermore, when the children come into the classroom, we behave towards them in a certain way, praise them for certain things, applaud generosity, encourage kindness, dissuade from bullying, and in this way, too, we are teaching. If, indeed, we are not aware that we are teaching at this point, then our influence could become dangerous through the very fact that we are unaware of what we are doing. One teacher I knew ensured that children used the colours he approved of in their pictures by surreptitiously taking away some colours and replacing them by others when they were not looking. If we do the same with our moral views we are close to indoctrination.

The emotional side of one's nature receives much attention from the progressive. To see it as erring and wayward, thwarting our reason, it is argued, is to look on its bad side. It has a good side. Our feelings may be ones of contentment and happiness, and this is something to be

97

valued. Why should we not be happy learning? Why should children not learn things that make them happy? (Is this the same question?) Certainly, there is no virtue in unhappiness. It seems to me sound to argue that you should not have to justify happiness, only unhappiness. But even if you accept that, there are still many questions left unanswered. For example, we can be happy about many things: sunbathing, collecting stamps, gardening, reading detective stories. It may be true that we learn better if we are happy doing something but it is still necessary to decide whether some ways of being happy are not better than others. That is, we cannot escape the question of value. One further word here. It is a mistake to think that different activities bring one the same kind of happiness. It is not quite like taking different routes and getting to the same place; for, in that case, the description of the destination is the same by no matter which route one arrived there. One's pleasure in playing the piano, however, is different from that gained in working out a mathematical puzzle. The kind of happiness one felt would be the result of the activity which had produced it, and one could only describe it with reference to this.

The progressive teacher is seen as the one who does not want children to sit still at their desks but to be active in doing, exploring, finding out, making. As adults we often discover that it is not until we have tried something out for ourselves that we really understand what is involved, and so there is a great deal of truth in the expression 'no understanding without doing'. Visiting the local church, factory or shopping centre is much more likely to bring understanding than its description alone. Even so, just visiting a place does not amount to a real experience of it. Hence the value of a talk by the curator of a museum to which we are taking the children, or a warden of a nature reserve, for without it the children might think that the one is an elaborate Oxfam shop and the other no more than a collection of weeds and trees with a few birds. Experience, then, must go hand-in-hand with tuition if learning is to take place.

Another way by which the freedom of the child is provided for is an environment which is 'informal', that of the traditional classroom being 'formal'. Most people regard these two words as opposites, again adding to the language of 'either—or' that Dewey spoke against. It is true that a classroom cannot be informal and formal at the same time, but it can be more or less formal or informal. These words admit of degree. They lie on a continuum or sliding scale. To say, therefore, that a class is either formal or informal gives us little information as it may lie in any of a number of places on that continuum. More knowledge, here again, is needed of the character and degree of the form it has.

A related word, which is confused with formal, is the word 'uniform'. The activity of a class could be described as formal and uniform when the teacher has arranged that all the pupils do the same thing in the same way together, as, say, in a lesson on handwriting. But a class may be formal without its activity being uniform. In topic work, by explicit directions or the use of work cards, the activity has been structured through groups or individuals in the class doing different (non-uniform) activities. The teaching is no less formal because the structure contains variety. Yet the kind of classroom which has children doing different tasks is often wrongly called informal or progressive. What degree of formality you decide on in the class will, of course, depend on the children and what you are teaching. Listening to a schools broadcast, say, on the Elizabethan Period would be formal, though follow-up work may be informal. Creative writing would be informal, but common errors of style and grammar may be tackled formally.

Conclusion

To sum up, an example may help the reader to see the differences between the two approaches to education, traditional and progressive, and the possibilities that lie between them. If we taught two children how to play chess, we might do it in one of three ways. First, we might tell them the rules and get them to repeat them back to us. We would then tell them to place the pieces on the board, stand behind them, and looking over their shoulders, tell them what moves to make. 'Place that pawn here', and 'Now the queen there.' We would, that is, direct the whole operation and the children would never be able to play on their own. Our second way would be to give the children the pieces and the board and suggest to them that they could play if they so wished. Of course, they would have no idea what the pieces stood for, what they were allowed to do and how to make successful moves. They could not even start to play the game. A third way, which you may have anticipated, is to tell them a few of the rules, set them to playing a simple game and without expecting too much, especially of a slow child, encourage them to make some moves of their own whilst suggesting others yourself. In this way you would ensure that they learned the rules; that is, that they avoided moves which were not allowed but developed the capacity to choose from those that were. It became their own game. Paradoxically, they were now free to play chess because they had been taught. The major differences between the traditionalist and progressive conceptions of teaching can be seen in this example. At one extreme the teacher is so concerned with the child's learning the rules and following them that no consideration is given to his point of view. At the other extreme, the teacher is so concerned with avoiding making the child do something against his present wishes that he takes away from him the chance of developing new ones.

It seems that the traditional teacher and the progressive teacher have a good deal to learn from each other. The use of the two labels has done great harm to education, for the two groups have many beliefs and practices in common, though there are some distinct differences as well. It is a mark of maturity in a teacher that he can preserve what he has learned by experience to be good and, at the same time, be flexible enough to make use of valuable innovations. It is only when we can free ourselves from labels and slavish adherence to any single doctrine that we can reach that maturity.

Further reading

The purpose of this chapter has not been to give a detailed account of the differences between traditional and progressive education, as nothing can take the place of numerous historical works which cover the last century. Two books that bring out the complexity of the ideas of this period are by R. J. W. Selleck, *New Education: the English Background, 1870 – 1914,* Pitman, 1968, and *English Primary Education and the Progressives, 1914 – 1939,* Routledge & Kegan Paul, 1972.

H. J. Entwistle's *Child-centred Education,* Methuen, 1970, offers a sympathetic examination of progressive education. More particularly the relation of happiness to education is considered by R. F. Dearden in 'Happiness as an Educational Aim', in *Education and the Development of Reason,* ed. R. F. Dearden, P. H. Hirst and R. S. Peters, Routledge & Kegan Paul, 1972.

What may be called the left-wing view of education does not belong to either the traditional or progressive approach. I. Illich's *De-schooling Society,* Open Forum, Penguin 1971, and his article 'The De-schooling of Society', in *Alternatives in Education,* University of London Press, 1973, show the radical character of his objections to the existing educational system.

Bibliography

BLISHEN, E. (1969), *Encyclopaedia of Education,* Blond.
BOARD OF EDUCATION (1931), *Report of the Consultative Committee on the Primary School* (Hadow Report), HMSO.
DEWEY, J. (1963), *Education and Experience,* Collier-Macmillan.
PETERS, R. S. (1965), *Ethics and Education,* Allen & Unwin.
SALMON, D. (1914), *The Art of Teaching,* Longman.
SKIDELSKY, R. (1969), *English Progressive Schools,* Penguin.

Chapter nine

Creativity

M.A.B. Degenhardt

It is pretty much taken for granted nowadays that a very, if not the most, important task of the teacher is to foster his or her pupils' powers of creativity. In all sorts of ways adventurous modern schools seek to give their pupils scope and encouragement to be more creative; and psychologists' researches into the nature of creativity are often designed to help them do this more effectively. It is easy to forget the relative newness of this enthusiasm: and it can come as a surprise to learn that the very word 'creativity' has only recently found its way into English dictionaries.

It is sometimes said that the study of history can be a very liberating exercise in that by inviting us to study and understand sympathetically past points of view which may be very different from our own, it brings us to see that there are elements in our own thinking which are wrongly taken for granted as obvious and unquestionable. The case of creativity is a good illustration of this point.

I remember seeing a photograph of an art lesson in an English elementary school of about the year 1900. The children were being taught to draw a leaf which the teacher had pinned in a top corner of the blackboard. And in the centre of the board he was drawing a large outline copy of the leaf shape. Meanwhile every boy in the class was carefully imitating the teacher's movements so as to duplicate the teacher's drawing on to his own paper. The teacher's chalk was half-way down the right hand side of his leaf, and every pupil's pencil was half-way down the right hand side of his leaf. No pupil was drawing from the actual leaf; no one was allowed any individual initiative as to *how* he drew a leaf, let alone any choice as to whether he drew a leaf or something else. The teacher was master of the skill of visual representation; the aim of the lesson was to have pupils master this skill by meticulously imitating the master.

This is a single example, but it is not too untypical of much that went on not only in the nineteenth-century English elementary school tradition, but in much other education of the past. No doubt comparably formal and stereotyped learning methods are still used, but with increasing success educators are urging the desirability of teaching situations in which children are encouraged to follow their own interests and initiative, to develop and exercise their individual talents, and to create something that is very much their own.

It would, of course, be wrong to suggest that education in the past was never concerned to make pupils creative. The old English grammar schools taught standards of good poetry and literature so that pupils would learn to write without offending against these standards. The student at a medieval university had to slave over the texts of classic philosophers, but he was not awarded his Doctor's degree until he could stand up in public to develop and defend his own philosophy; Sir Joshua Reynolds as first president of the Royal Academy (1769–90), required 'that an implicit obedience to the *Rules of Art*, as established by the practice of the great MASTERS, should be exacted from the young students' (Reynolds, 1961 ed., p. 21), because he was convinced that only then was there any chance that they in their turn would become great. But in all this there is an important difference from the typical modern approach; for whereas the older style of thinker tended to the view that only a specially gifted few could become creative, and even then only after a long spell of submission to a pretty demanding educational programme, the modern enthusiast aspires for all his pupils to achieve creativity right now. This surely is much more exciting; children's lives are to be enriched while they are still in school by the experience of being creative, and this experience is not to be the prerogative of a select few. The new approach, then, represents a considerable advance: or does it? The more traditional educator might see it as a serious mistake, and we will better understand both approaches if we ask why he might think this.

First, he might suggest that modern approaches seriously devalue the notion of 'creativity'. In the past this word itself seems not to have been used; but people did talk of 'creating' and 'creations', and great artists were labelled 'creative'. But such words apply to something special. When we call Beethoven, or Turner, or Einstein creative we are putting them in a class of very remarkable people; of people, that is, who are distinguished by their remarkable works. And when we contemplate such works, when we contemplate, for example, a powerful symphony, a fine painting or a revolutionary body of scientific theory, we are profoundly impressed, even overwhelmed by this work as the product of an outstanding individual talent combined with much industry and application. Nor is it just for the moment that we are impressed; one measure of a work's greatness is that we can return to it again and again to discover in it new features, values, relations and significances.

All this being so, the 'traditionalist' might argue, do we not seriously mislead ourselves when we confidently apply the word creativity to, for example, the lesson where the teacher plays the class a piece of exotic music and everyone writes down the thoughts it immediately engenders; or where, at a moment's notice, children improvise dramatisations of fairy stories or scenes from their daily lives. Our 'traditionalists' will perhaps recognise some value in these activities; the children's writings and improvisations may display charm and insight, and the exercise may foster confidence, fluency and awareness. But he is likely to protest at putting these achievements in the same category as a poem by Donne or a performance by Olivier; and he might doubt whether such undisciplined activities are even of much value in educating children towards becoming really creative in the demanding sense in which he understands the word.

In reply to this the 'progressive' teacher will have formidable arguments available. He will claim that rather than stifle creativity, as in so much traditional schooling, his approach will foster it by making maximum allowance for pupils' individual differences, encouraging them to follow up their own special interests, and giving them scope to develop their own unique talents. His lessons allow every child to enjoy for himself the experience of being creative; which, as well as being valuable in itself, will surely help him to appreciate the creative experiences of others. He might add arguments to do with children's mental health rather than their education, for many therapists believe that the pursuit of free creative activities can help us resolve mental tensions and disorders.

Our 'traditionalist' might now reply that to think on these lines is to miss the whole point of education. To be educated, he will say, is to come to share in that heritage of knowledge and understanding which mankind has accumulated, and which enables us to interpret experience and make something of our lives. Human life can become enriched only in so far as it is informed by the cultural inheritance that mankind has accumulated over many centuries. The job of education is to pass on this inheritance, not to foster merely natural developments nor to indulge individual whims and preferences. And the knowledge that composes this inheritance is not easily come by; indeed, the fact that we organise it into 'disciplines' is a healthy reminder that the privilege of enjoying it has to be won by disciplining ourselves to work to rigorous standards and master difficult materials. Children may greatly enjoy being taught by modern creativity methods; but we should not think we are doing them a favour by neglecting to give them the real stuff of education.

Now this imaginary debate could, of course, go on, and on . . . and on. But perhaps an important point has already become clear: debate about creativity methods in education does not stand all on its own;

rather it is very much tied up with some of the huge controversial issues that *must* confront anyone who approaches modern schooling in a lively and inquiring way. Such questions, for example, as whether we should give children more freedom to follow their individual bents and initiative, or be firmer in requiring them to master established bodies of learning, or whether education is best seen as the drawing out of individual potentialities, or the passing on of a human inheritance. The topic of creativity in education should, then, be worth looking into not just in its own right, but also for the light it may throw on these wider issues.

I have suggested that many modern ideas on creativity fit in comfortably with what *today* counts as a very progressive approach to education: but in chapter 8 in this volume it is suggested that a sounder understanding of education results from a constructive synthesis between these two approaches. In line with this I shall try to show how a sounder understanding of creativity will help the working teacher integrate into his approach valuable insights from both the traditional and the progressive views of education.

In recent years the researches of psychologists have sought to throw light on the nature of creativity. But there is much scope for philosophy to supplement and co-operate in this inquiry, the psychologist being concerned to research the facts of the case, the philosopher to sort out those puzzles about creativity which simply cannot be solved by looking to the factual evidence; those puzzles, that is, which require us to look more carefully at the meaning of our terms and the logic of our arguments. In the first instance philosophy ought to help us be a bit clearer and more precise about what 'creativity' means (surely a very urgent task in view of the way some educational writers apply the term to just about *any* educational innovations that they approve of, so threatening to deprive it of any real meaning). With this clarification behind us we can go on to reflect on how creativity is achieved and what connection, if any, it has with education.

One should not, however, expect too much from a brief philosophical scrutiny. The ability to create has often been represented as a very remarkable, and uniquely human, characteristic: it is hardly likely to yield its secrets easily to philosopher or to psychologist.

One can distinguish two ways of looking at creativity, and these can be conveniently labelled the 'inner' and the 'outer'. One approach takes it that what is important is the 'inner' mental process, or private personal experience of being creative, and the other concentrates on the created end product (painting, poem, invention, theory or whatever) which is publicly observable or 'outer'. Both approaches have proved their value; but it does seem to be a rather common logical error to *start* from the 'inner' approach, for whatever else the word 'create' means, it surely implies that something is, in fact, created. We would surely not talk of someone being creative, or having a creative experience, and then go on to say that he did not create anything. A philosopher might put this point by saying that while, of course, the creative process is temporally prior to the created end product, nevertheless the created end product is logically prior to the creative process – for it is only in so far as there is a created end product that we can identify a process (or indeed, a person) as creative. To use what has become a standard illustration of this point, we know very little about the man Shakespeare (in fact there is some doubt as to who he was); yet we are rightly confident in our judgment that he was highly creative, because we are familiar with his plays and poems – that is, with his creations. (This is not, of course, to deny that it would be interesting to know more about the man Shakespeare and his mental processes. We might then learn much about how he became creative, but *nothing* more about *whether* he was creative.)

I may seem to have been labouring this horribly obvious point that to talk of 'creating' implies that something is created; but obvious or not the point needs to be laboured simply because so many theorists seem to forget it.

Attending then to end products, let us now ask what kind of end products justify talk of creativity? Helpful in this respect is R. K. Elliott's paper 'Changing concepts of creativity' (Elliott, 1971) in which he distinguishes a traditional concept of creativity very much rooted in the fine arts from a newer concept at home in all areas of human knowledge and activity.

The traditional concept

The traditional concept sees the artist as creative by analogy to God in the Genesis account. Just as the Biblical God called into being or created an entirely new existence, i.e. the world, so, it is suggested, the artist calls into being an entirely new existence (some even say a new world) in the form of a work of art. This concept can be traced back at least to the view of the seventeenth-century Polish poet and theorist, Father Kazimierez Maciej Sarbienski, that the essence of poetry is an imaginative fiction; the poet, like God, constructs and creates his new work, so that every poem is, as it were, a world of its own (Osborne, 1968, p. 93).

An interesting modern variation of this view is argued by the contemporary American philosopher Suzanne Langer in the chapter on 'Creation' in her book *Problems of Art* (1957). She asks why we speak of creating a painting, a dance or a poem, but of making or manufacturing automobiles, bricks, aluminium pots, toothpaste and shoes. Her answer (p. 28) is that:

an ordinary object, say a shoe, is made by putting pieces of leather together; the pieces were there before. The shoe is a construction of leather. It has a special shape and use and name, but it is still an article of leather and is thought of as such. A picture is made by deploying pigments on a piece of canvas, but the picture is not a pigment-and-canvas structure. The picture that emerges from the process is a structure of space, and the space itself is an emergent whole of shapes, visible colored volumes. Neither the space nor the things in it were in the room before. Pigments and canvas are not in the pictorial space: they are in the space of the room as they were before.

At first sight this concept of creativity would seem to have no application outside the field of the arts; and if this is so it is a mistake to speak, as we often do speak, of creativity in the sciences. To say this is not to rate the arts above the sciences, so threatening to spark off one of those tedious arts *v.* sciences debates: it is merely to pin-point an important difference. The artist, being centrally concerned to create, adds something quite new to the world that can now be contemplated with delight or wonder. The scientist is centrally concerned with truth, and with the discovery of more facts about the world as it already is; discoveries which, too, may yield a different kind of wonder and delight.

However, the contrast is not really quite so simple. For while it may be true that the scientist is typically concerned to add new facts to the accumulation of human knowledge, those scientists who make outstanding impacts often do something very different: the importance of, say, a Newton, a Darwin, a Karl Marx or an Einstein is not so much that their researches have unearthed new pieces of information, as that they have suggested to us a new way of 'seeing' or understanding the data we already have available. Some scientists, that is, change our picture of the world to such an extent that it seems appropriate to say that they have re-created our world, or created a new world for us.

Perhaps I can illustrate this point from the career of one scientist. As a young researcher, Sigmund Freud first made his mark when he located the apparently recondite testes of the common eel. He was rightly commended for this discovery — but it would have been odd to call him 'creative' for locating what were already there. Indeed, to have used the label in this context might have offended Freud by suggesting that he was either an impostor or a practical joker who, failing to locate the testes, had manufactured substitutes.

Later in his career, however, Freud put together an abundance of known facts (some of which he had himself discovered) in his theory of the unconscious: a theory which, if accepted, so radically changed existing ways of thinking about mankind that it would seem appropriate to say that Freud had done more than discover new truths about the human psyche — he had created a new image of man.

The new concept

The new concept of creativity is seen by Elliott as having come into prominence in the post-war era in a context where nuclear and space-research programmes presented a variety of theoretical and technical problems to the solution of which traditional ways of thinking seemed inadequate. This concept of creativity has a much wider application, being used of any case where someone comes up with new ideas, either by way of solution to a hitherto intransigent problem, or to be developed in their own right. Here there is not so much a new concept as a new label, the word creative now being used to cover what used to be covered by *one* meaning of the older expression 'imaginative'. In this sense it would be appropriate to call someone creative (or imaginative) who, for example, invented a clever gadget, saw an unconventional way round a technological block, devised an original military strategy, innovated an artistic style or framed an exciting scientific hypothesis.

Clearly this is a concept of creativity which is appropriate and at home in any area of human thought or activity.

A third concept?

Do Elliott's two concepts together cover all important uses of the term 'creativity'? There seems to me to be at least one other sense, and a specifically educational sense, of the word in contemporary usage.

In education (and particularly, though not exclusively, in the education of younger children) we encounter much talk of 'creative activities', 'creative work', 'creative play' and the like, where the emphasis does not seem to be on any created end product: something of merit may or may not be created, but this does not seem to be centrally important. It seems, rather, that these goings on earn the label 'creative' by virtue of something in their manner — their being characterised by their allowing great individual freedom and initiative to pupils, by their not just permitting, but encouraging, each pupil to pursue his own interests, develop his own ideas, express his own feelings and personality.

One does not have to know very much about modern psychology and educational theory to see that there are good grounds for believing in the value of such activities in terms both of children's education and their mental health. (Nor, of course, does one have to think very hard to see why it might be a serious mistake to have children do this sort of thing all day and every day.) It does, however, seem rather odd to use the label 'creative' here, precisely because of the lack of emphasis on anything being created. (One might, I suppose, say that children are 'creating themselves', but this, one would hope, must be true of all education.)

If I am right to suggest that this use of the word 'creative' is not really appropriate, then we can concentrate our attention on Elliott's two senses, and consider what light philosophy can throw on how we might seek to educate for creativity thus understood. Now both these senses or concepts of creativity that Elliott has discerned to be in use have important features in common (which no doubt helps to explain why they are not always easily distinguished, and why the same word is used to cover them both). In either sense, where someone is creative he achieves something new, and something that is held to be of value; and he does this deliberately or intentionally. Here then, it can be said, are three criteria which any act or performance must satisfy if it is to earn the label creative: it must intentionally bring about something that is both novel and valuable. It will throw much light on the possibility of educating for creativity if we look at these three criteria in more detail.

1   What is created must be novel — at any rate to the creator. We might say that the unknown inventor of the first brick was creative — but not so the production line worker turning out his hundredth brick of the day. Van Gogh was creative when he painted a southern landscape, but not the man who correctly fills in the numbered squares in an outline copy of this landscape. 'Ximenes' creates crossword puzzles: but we only solve them.

2   What is created must be judged to be of some value. It is, of course, true that we sometimes use expressions like 'Who created that mess?' or 'Stop creating that row'; but these seem to be rather untypical (perhaps even ironic) usages. Normally we wouldn't talk of creating, unless what was created was held to be of some value. (Of course the judgment of value might be mistaken: but we use the word 'creative' when approval *seems* to be appropriate.)

3   What is created must be intentionally created. To say this is not to deny that the element of chance may be important, as in the case of some famous invention, or in various modern developments in the arts which deliberately make use of random factors. It is, however, to insist that the agent must have a pretty good idea of what he is doing. (This criterion can raise important and interesting questions in education that are too difficult to go into here, but that may repay further discussion. Young children often produce strikingly beautiful paintings, or put words together in an exciting way. How are we to judge the extent to which these are the products of deliberate intention or lucky accident?)

If these criteria are correct, then they would seem to throw valuable light on questions about how to educate for creativity. Let us look at criteria 2 and 3 in this respect before returning to look at criterion 1. These two criteria together suggest that creativity implies the intentional production of something valuable: and this means that the creator must himself have a good grasp of the appropriate values. But to say this raises a host of difficult philosophical puzzles about the nature and justification of values. Clearly to judge, say, a painting or a new scientific theory, we must bring values and standards to bear. But where do these values come from? And what measure of objectivity is it reasonable to claim for them? Few philosophers today would be prepared to defend the notion that there are absolute, objective values which are somehow just given, and which we just have to accept. But neither is it very satisfactory to go to the other extreme, and say that judgments of value are entirely personal and subjective, matters of individual whim and fancy: for if we abandoned all values in this way we might have to cease making any distinction between creativity and arbitrary action.

The advocate of this sort of highly relativistic viewpoint is likely to defend it by pointing to the great amount of disagreement between people when they make value judgments. If we always disagree in our estimate of, say, a work of art, how, he asks, can we suppose that our value judgments will ever be anything but highly subjective? One possible and important answer to this point is to note that when we disagree about, for example, whether Picasso's 'blue period' was marred by sentimentality, or whether some critics have over-rated D. H. Lawrence, we do know what we are disagreeing about. Does not this suggest that underlying even our most vehement disagreements there must be important, if not very explicit, agreement on fundamentals? Indeed, if this were not the case it is hard to see how a meaningful disagreement could be possible.

This point seems to indicate a way out of the dilemma, though here there is only space to sketch the broad outlines of an answer.

If someone is creative, he is creative *at* something — at say, composing music, devising geometrical demonstrations or framing scientific hypotheses. He is, that is to say, involved in some activity that defines and gives meaning to what he is doing. An interesting thing about these activities (e.g. art, mathematics, science) is that we would probably find it hard to achieve an agreed definition of them: and certainly we would find it impossible to achieve a definition that would be at all informative or helpful to anyone who did not already have a pretty good idea of what art or mathematics or science was. A man might have a rich understanding of the nature of art, but wisely refrain from telling us what it is. The explanation of this paradox seems to be in the notion of a tradition. Art becomes recognisable as art, and science becomes recognisable as science, when a tradition of such activity has emerged: that is, when man has begun to engage in a variety of activities which can be grouped together under the label of art, or science or whatever because they are thought about in the same sort of way and described in the same sort of language. Normally one acquires some grasp of the nature of these activities when, in the process of growing-up, one is initiated into the appropriate ways of acting, thinking and talking that constitute a particular tradition. One does not, that is to say, learn what art is from formal definitions of art, but by enjoying works of art, listening to and participating in the appropriate ways of talking about them, and perhaps even engaging in their production. To make sense of such experience is to be initiated into a tradition of art. In learning about that tradition one also learns the values that are part of it — although one may never be able to make them fully explicit.

From all this it follows that part of the task of education for creativity must be to initiate people into the appropriate tradition, so that they come to understand the nature of the activity in which they are to engage, and to recognise and care for the standards and values appropriate to it. By this I mean not, say, that we should give children a potted history of science: but that, over a period of time, we should ensure that they have sufficient experience of scientific activity and discourse to acquire a good working idea of what science is all about; they must, that is, come to be able to think scientifically or within the scientific tradition.

But all this talk of 'tradition' may seem rather strange, for the word tradition often carries with it suggestions of being confined and restricted to the past and to past achievements in a manner altogether antithetical to the notion of creativity. Certainly we do often talk of 'tradition' and 'traditional' in this way; but there is nothing necessarily hidebound and restrictive about a tradition. We also often, and rightly, talk of a 'living' tradition; a tradition that builds on past achievements in order to grow and innovate.

The importance of tradition is well illustrated in the history of the visual arts where even the most radical innovators have been immeasurably indebted to what they have learned in the tradition in which they have grown up. Indeed, if this were not so, there would be no such thing as the artistic style of a region or an epoch. It is the tradition which gives even the greatest artist a starting point from which to make his unique contribution. Some artists, of course, innovate so radically that contemporaries find it hard to make very much sense of their work, or to relate it to the kind of art with which they are familiar. But the interesting point is that with the passage of time they learn to see the innovator's work as related to what has gone before: and in so doing they come to make more of it.

The reader will readily see that much of what I have just been saying holds equally well of areas of human activity other than the arts.

Talk of innovation within a tradition brings me back to the 'novelty' criterion of creativity: but before looking at this in a little detail I want to suggest that the important elements of mastery and understanding of which I have been talking so far are much neglected, and dangerously so, by many contemporary educationalists — whether they be psychometrists who devise creativity tests which award marks for mere novelty, without seeking evidence of value and understanding, or classroom practitioners who fear to do any positive educating of their pupils lest they stifle their creativity. Here it seems to me, the 'progressive' teacher has much to learn from that concern for standards and mastery which typified his 'traditionalist' predecessor.

The mistakes I have been talking of may be dangerous, but they are hardly foolish. It is easy to see how one is led into them by being over-concerned with the novelty aspect of creativity, which I now want to look at. If we ask what the teacher can do by way of teaching the element of novelty, we get the possibly surprising answer 'nothing'. But that creativity cannot be taught is surely true by definition in so far as when we say a child has been creative, we mean that he has innovated, that he has contributed something new of his own, that he has gone beyond what we have taught him. If we *had* taught it to him it would have been neither an innovation, nor creative.

However, this important linguistic point is not as devastating as might first appear. It certainly does not imply that we must dismiss all notions of creativity as an educational aim. To suggest that talk of teaching creativity is a contradiction in terms is quite consistent with the suggestion that we can and should be concerned to know what kinds of teaching are most likely to favour the emergence of creativity.

It is worth comparing these points with what the eighteenth-century Prussian philosopher Immanuel Kant had to say about genius (Kant, 1790, 1972 ed., §46–50). A work of art, he argues, is dependent on some rules which can be taught and learned; but beautiful things cannot be produced merely by acting according to definite rules. Genius, then, is the talent for going beyond the rules and producing that for which no definite rule can be given — but since it will not do for genius to produce original nonsense, its products must be exemplary models which can serve to give new rules and standards for others.

What now becomes clear, and this *is* problematic for the teacher, is that education for creativity requires apparently conflicting, if not incompatible emphases. On the one hand, I have argued, the teacher must exert himself to pass on to the pupil an already established body of knowledge and standards, and he must pass this on in such a way that the pupil comes to care about, and be influenced by it. On the other hand the pupil must not be unduly restricted or inhibited by what we teach him, for to achieve creativity he must go beyond this and create something of his own. (This, surely, is where the traditionalist has much to learn from the progressive teacher's concern to avoid such inhibiting effects.)

Apart then from providing children with challenges and opportunities to be creative, the teacher aiming at creativity must be continually looking for ways to teach which combine a maximum of passing on with a minimum of restriction. Of course, every thoughtful teacher will know that there are a number of ways, varying between subjects and age-groups, in which this can be done; but two examples may helpfully illustrate the sort of thing I have in mind.

1   In teaching art we should, at some stage, begin to acquaint children with the work of outstanding artists: but some educationalists might have reasonable fears lest we impose on children one particular set of aesthetic values. Why not then show children works in a range and variety of styles (encouraging them to discuss and compare these) so that they come both to grasp aesthetic values, and to see that these values are richly variable, adaptable and ever evolving.

2   In teaching science a similar point might hold. Typically, we tend to concentrate on teaching only scientific theories having contemporary currency, thus, perhaps, suggesting that while new scientific knowledge is constantly accumulating, it does so within a relatively fixed theoretical framework. But is it not important to help pupils to see science as having a history: a history in which the constant change of viewpoint, and the exploration of new ways of looking at things, is of vital importance. And if this is so, might it not be more important than is generally realised to include something of the history of the subject in science education, taking pains to achieve a sympathetic presentation of 'outmoded' theories such that pupils see why now abandoned viewpoints were once convincing and helpful.

But I suspect that teaching manner is at least as important as content; the teaching manner, that is, which encourages in children an intelligently critical confidence in the value of their own efforts and initiative. Every teacher has his own style: but to display a style that stifles the emergence of such confidence in one's pupils is surely to fail as a teacher.

In this brief paper I have raised more contentious issues than I have been able to follow through. Let me, then, conclude by indicating some of the possible areas of fundamental disagreement with what I have said, in the hope that this will provide a basis for further discussion.

1   Against my view that education is important in the matter of creativity, the cynic might point out that people of little or bad education have often achieved outstanding creativity.

2   I have argued that it only makes sense to talk of being creative in the context of an already established set of values in terms of which we judge the created end product. On this ground I might be inclined to

laugh off those theorists who seem to think that creativity comes naturally bubbling out of the untutored mind. But am I being too cavalier with such views, and so neglecting important educational insights?

3 My biggest assumption has been that creativity *ought* to be an educational aim. But why should this be so? Much current interest in this area was born of concern in the USA that Russia took the initial lead in the 'Space Race'; and we often hear that business and industry need more creative talent. But surely we should be wary of letting such politico-economic considerations shape the curricula of children in school.

Of course, many enthusiasts regard creativity as something due to the individual pupil. Creativity, they might say, is a good not for the society but for the child who achieves it. But can these theorists answer the critic who says, 'Look, why should being creative be regarded as the great human privilege? Man already has available to him a vast body of creative achievements: and he must be educated if he is to enjoy these. Should not this be the teacher's main concern?'

Further reading

In this chapter I have been very dependent on two papers which seem to me to be indispensable reading on this topic. These papers are R. K. Elliott's 'Changing concepts of creativity' (see Bibliography), and J. P. White's 'Creativity and education: a philosophical analysis', *British Journal of Educational Studies*, June 1968, republished in R. F. Dearden, P. H. Hirst and R. S. Peters (eds), *Education and the Development of Reason*, Routledge & Kegan Paul, 1972. (To this I am indebted when I suggest criteria which must be satisfied if the label 'creative' is to be accurately applied.)

Probably the best summary guide to the psychological research on creativity is still Moya Tyson's paper 'Creativity' in B. Foss (ed.), *New Horizons in Psychology*, Penguin, 1966.

The importance of a tradition to creativity in the visual arts is well brought out in the writings on art history of E. H. Gombrich: see particularly chapters V and IX of his *Art and Illusion*, Phaidon, 1960.

The kind of practical approach to teaching for creativity that I recommend is not, of course, new as is shown in Marion Richardson's descriptions of her own teaching methods in her *Art and the Child*, London University Press, 1948.

Bibliography

ELLIOTT, R. K. (1971), 'Changing concepts of creativity', *Proceedings of the Philosophy of Education Society of Great Britain*, vol. V, no. 2.

M. A. B. Degenhardt

KANT, I. (1790; 1972 ed.), *Critique of Judgment,* trans. J. H. Bernard, Hafner Publishing.
LANGER, S. (1957), *Problems of Art*, Routledge & Kegan Paul.
OSBORNE, H. (1968), *Aesthetics and Art Theory*, Longman.
REYNOLDS, Sir JOSHUA (1961 ed.), *Discourses on Art*, ed. R. W. Wark, Collier-Macmillan.

Chapter ten

Freedom

F. M. Berenson

Let us begin with a statement which I take to be unequivocal, given a society like our democracy: 'It is desirable that all men should be free.' The statement is unequivocal because it is expressed in rather a mild form. Had I used the stronger term 'necessary' instead of 'desirable' then objections could be raised as to possibilities of an individual being free. What sort of objections would these be? Perhaps we can answer this by an example: A teacher is confronted with a 'difficult' pupil, John. He complains that there is nothing he can do with John because John has been conditioned, or has formed strong habits, or has been unduly influenced by social factors, or is psychologically so mixed up that he has refused or is unable to respond, cannot control his objectionable behaviour and so on. It is not all that important, for our purposes, precisely how the teacher describes the situation; whichever of the above descriptions he chooses will depend to a large extent on his background learning. What is important is the general point the teacher is making, namely that John has become so set in certain ways of behaviour that nothing can be done to counteract them. Thus neither John nor the teacher are free to act, John in particular *cannot help* being the problem pupil he is. He has been caused or determined by his background and past experiences to act in a certain way and is no longer free to act differently. On the face of it, it looks as if we cannot be free agents if we are determined. From what I have said about John, it also follows that, since we all have our particular backgrounds and past experiences, we also are in that sense determined to act in certain ways rather than others. To what extent then can we be said to have a free choice to act one way rather than another? To answer this question we need to take a brief look at one particular theory of determinism and its implications for freedom as such. This theory carries with it vital implications both for the bringing up and educating of children. We shall then go on to consider the concept of freedom. First, then, some explanation is needed of the term 'determinism'. To determine something is to put bounds to, to fix, to limit, etc. Determinism, which stems from this notion, is a doctrine which claims that all things about man, including his will, are determined or fixed by certain causes. Thus everything that happens, every event or every human action is caused in a way such that the outcome is a necessary one and *could not* be otherwise. Thus a necessary connection is set up between causes and their effects over which men have little or no control as regards their actions or choices. Now it will be seen, if the above is the case, that freedom becomes an empty notion because man, on this view, is no longer responsible for what he does — he cannot act otherwise than he does. The implications for any notion of freedom in general and say, moral responsibility in particular, are very formidable. But there are several different theories of determinism and only some of these stand in opposition to the possibility of freedom, others try to reconcile the two notions. I shall concentrate on only one of the basic theories of determinism - namely psychological determinism as this particular theory carries with it very significant consequences for the teacher.

Psychological determinism

Theories which fall under this heading stem from the doctrine known as dualism. Descartes, for instance, made a sharp distinction between minds and bodies as two entirely distinct substances with utterly distinct and different essential qualities. His theory raised difficulties about how these two separate and distinct substances could interact in a person and thus much of Descartes's philosophy has come to be rejected, but the important distinction has been preserved with certain important modifications. The modifications in contemporary philosophy turn on the point that mind and body are no longer held to be distinct and essentially different substances. The distinction is drawn instead between what can be said or attributed to the mind and what to the body. Thus a distinction is drawn between 'psychological' predicates on the one hand and 'physical' predicates on the other. Psychological predicates express what pertains to the mind (e.g. he hopes, thinks, dislikes, etc.), and physical predicates that which pertains to the body (e.g. he is 6 feet tall, has a quick walk, is sitting, bending down, etc.). Because the distinction is drawn in terms of psychological predicates which apply to human behaviour, most modern theories of this kind are usually known as theories of psychological determinism. Thus acts of will, desires, emotions, i.e. the class of things to which psychological predicates apply, are taken in modern theories of psychological determinism to be psychological or mental events within the mind of the agent. These psychological or mental events, which govern our behaviour, are in turn governed and caused by unconscious forces, defences and such like which stem from our childhood experiences and background. In most cases we are quite unaware of any of these causes — they are followed by their effects in the form of our behaviour which we often cannot control. Now, the problem arises that an agent's actions which are causally determined can be seen as 'free' only in a technical sense which does not correspond with the notion of freedom that men in fact have and which is essential for holding a man morally (or legally) responsible for his actions. A genuinely free action, therefore, must be one not simply caused by one's desires but one which can also be avoided, in that the agent could still have done otherwise than he did. This can be illustrated by an example (Taylor, 1967).

Supposing we have a pupil in the top form of a secondary school who is constantly stealing from others in the class. Now, in accordance with determinism, as he always steals when prompted by his desires and provided that his efforts meet with no impediment his actions are, therefore, free and voluntary and he is responsible for them. But now let us carry this further, still in keeping with determinism. Suppose that he has no control over his motives which arise as a result of a terrible background and deprivation in childhood. In other words, he is simply the product of influences which feed his motives and in turn *make him* steal. Anti-determinists would argue here that given his background he still did not have to become a thief as many others from similar backgrounds never steal. But for determinists this would be unacceptable because they would have to say that his actions were causally determined and, therefore, inevitable and unavoidable. It follows that he cannot help being what he is and acting as he does. On this view no man can be held responsible for his actions and therefore questions of morality and hence of praise, blame and punishment do not arise. Here then we get some obviously startling consequences for the teacher. But what is, perhaps, less obvious is that the teacher can be seen as causing to a significant degree the very influences which will make the pupil what he will become. One's reaction to this is a disturbing realisation of the responsibility the teacher has to bear. But does he? Well, the answer, on this thesis, is a definite 'no' because the teacher's behaviour is in turn caused by his background and so on.

It can, I hope, be seen from the above why many philosophers have fought hard to resist this kind of psychological determinism. They argued and are arguing today that they do not wish to deny that we are influenced by our background and past experiences but at the same time man can and is in fact responsible for what he does. All our laws are based on rewards and punishment and rest on the assumption that men's motives can be relied upon to have some regular influence on their behaviour. To some extent we can predict how men will act in given circumstances. This sort of predictability is a necessary condition of our being able to communicate, necessary for forming personal relationships, for getting to know what a person is like. This condition of regularity is an important factor in enabling a teacher to get to know his pupils.

The contrast we have been discussing could, perhaps, be put as follows.

There are, in the main, two views regarding determinism:

1   Hard determinism which involves the thesis that man cannot help being what he is nor doing what he does and as a consequence moral assessment of his actions is irrational and cannot be seen as appropriate. As far as I know, very few philosophers seriously hold this thesis today. By contrast, many psychologists and psychiatrists do hold this view. Generally speaking, psychiatrists are rather irritated by theories of human freedom. They consider the question whether human behaviour is causally determined to be an empirical question of fact. They also claim to know what these causes are, especially in abnormal behaviour. On this view our choices, deliberations, desires, emotions and so on are governed or caused by unconscious forces or inner defences whose existence we ourselves do not even suspect. We are victims of what has been imposed on us in our earliest years by parents and others, episodes we don't even remember. In view of this, to speak of human behaviour as in any way free, is an illusion. My reaction here is one of puzzlement as to how the above conclusion can be taken as a matter of fact.

2   Soft determinism tries to reconcile some form of determinism with the possibility of applying moral judgments to a man's actions. One such attempt is to show that man is a cause of his own actions — that man can decide to act in a way which is *in opposition* to his desires and inclinations, act in a way he considers right or good. T. Reid (1969 ed.), among many other philosophers, argued very forcibly against hard determinism on the grounds that such a thesis goes very much against a whole range of beliefs held by men. When men constantly try to make decisions as to which way to act in a given situation, this presupposes the firm belief that there is a point to their deliberations, that while choosing action A, they were still free to perform action B. In this sense men are causes of their own actions, of their own behaviour. Reid saw this as the justification for calling a man an agent in that man is a being who acts in addition to being acted upon. The distinction at stake here is an important one. On the one hand we have man acting freely, on the other, man is caused to act by something outside himself. The latter can be compared to a machine which is switched on and set to perform in a certain specific way. Reid saw the latter as a contradiction when applied to men — something like a non-self-acting agent.

Determinism and the teacher

The two versions of determinism discussed above raise important issues for the teacher. As a result, the teacher today finds himself in a serious dilemma. On the one hand he thinks it a part of his task to help the pupil towards the development of a socially and morally well integrated personality and on the other hand the teacher is faced with a psychological theory which stresses that discipline of any kind is well-nigh useless because the actions of certain pupils cannot be controlled or corrected by the teacher nor even by the pupil himself. What is the teacher to do under the circumstances? We all, I think, accept that a number of children are greatly deprived in various ways. We also, I think, accept that children brought up in deprived circumstances become gravely affected by them in all sorts of ways ranging from behaviour problems to educational problems. But the vital point here is whether we also believe that something concrete can be done to counteract these unfortunate circumstances or whether we believe that all we can do is accept the state of affairs and do the best we can under the circumstances. The above is an extremely serious decision facing teachers today and for many, the latter alternative seems one which makes school life more viable. But, at the same time, there are serious attempts being made to solve many of these problems. Children needing attention in any way are given opportunities such as remedial reading, pursuit of their special interests and, perhaps, what is most important, they are made to feel that someone is taking a real interest in them as persons and in their individual difficulties. Most children, once the teacher has gained their confidence, will respond in all sorts of ways. They will be willing to accept the necessity of keeping certain rules provided they understand the rationale behind them. Deprived children are children on whom adults have constantly imposed in one way or another. Their freedom as persons has been curtailed because deprivation is a serious curtailment of freedom to live a normal life. I shall return to this point in greater detail but, for the present, I would stress that it is necessary to learn to be free. By this I mean that we have to come to understand that all rules are not merely impositions but that they are necessary for freedom to operate. Let us look at some examples.

A given school has a rule forbidding running along the corridors and staircases. The reason for this rule may be quite obvious to teachers but many pupils, particularly the deprived ones, often see it as yet another imposition and a curtailment of their freedom of movement and, therefore, as something to resist. We, as teachers, have no right to assume that what is self-evident to us is equally self-evident to our pupils. There is, therefore, a constant need for our being aware of circumstances which may lead to problems which are avoidable.

Another example here is that of the 'school uniform' controversy. There are a number of arguments which can be put forward such as that they do away with inequalities arising from some children being better dressed than others, that a uniform gives one a sense of belonging to a particular community with whom one can identify, that a uniform is designed for safety, etc. All the above are valid arguments but on the other hand we have arguments against uniforms which centre round the curtailment of freedom to dress as one likes, particularly at the level of top forms in secondary schools. It has been shown by various researches that children themselves, when this issue was discussed and the pros and cons pointed out to them, were divided in their opinions. The crux of the matter here is to guard against imposing rules which have a very thin justification and could, therefore, be dispensed with. The attitudes, aims and approach to these problems of any given teacher will depend on whether he accepts hard or soft determinism. I have offered examples based on the latter version. I do not wish to deny that we are influenced to a large extent by our past experiences, environment, hereditary factors and such like but, given all this, man has the power to refrain from acting from a very strong desire on either rational or moral grounds. What differentiates us in an important way from inanimate objects is that we are creatures capable of having intentions. We are capable of doing certain things in order to achieve certain specific results, we think of the best ways of achieving ends, although our ends may to a large extent depend on our particular interests. This separates us off from inanimate objects in an important way. Concepts like that of intention cannot be explained in terms of physics. There is nothing in the realm of physical science which corresponds to this. If we accept this view then it seems to me that man, although influenced by many external considerations which may shape his character, can still act freely, make decisions, choices and form intentions on which he acts. It also seems to me that causes which affect our actions can change because our desires, or views which we hold, change. This point seems crucial. I want to suggest that it is *because* our actions stem from various springs — caused or self-caused — that we often find it difficult to decide whether or not to hold an agent responsible for certain actions. Given this, what consequences follow for the practising teacher? The answers to this question are many. They raise problems about authority, the individual, the group and in addition questions about systems of education. I shall concentrate on what seems to me to be the central issue here, namely what is involved in claiming freedom for one's pupils? I shall not discuss the distinction between freedom and anarchy because by now, I think, we are all familiar with this. I shall, therefore, dismiss it in one sentence — we cannot enjoy freedom of any kind within a society without some rules devised to safeguard that freedom, whereas anarchy demands the abolition of any restrictions whatever, thereby allowing one individual to encroach on the freedom of others. We could think here of traffic lights — I am not free to drive on when the traffic lights are red but supposing we abolished all traffic lights, would we be able to drive freely?

A significant point to note is that the word 'free' has a commendatory force; it is prescriptive. By this I mean that it expresses approval when used. In addition, demands for freedom are often emotional in that they express a wish for the destruction of existing institutions and authority in general and in this the demands are rather empty because no specific constructive criticisms are made nor alternatives offered. The difficulty with the term 'free' is that it is used to describe many and varied things. In this respect it is very much like the term 'equal'. To say that all men should be free or that all men are equal is not saying anything which is very informative. We must also state in what respect they are to be free or equal, e.g. man demands to be free in respect of pursuing his job in the way he thinks best or in respect of having freedom of speech just as we say that two men are equal in respect of height or ability in mathematics. Now, what kinds of freedom can be specified? There are some very important distinctions to be made between different kinds of freedom. John Stuart Mill in his essay *On Liberty* (1859) defines freedom as absence of constraint and coercion. Thus freedom consists in an absence of constraint or coercion imposed by another person, the state or any other authority. A man is thus said to be free when he is in a position to choose his own ends, his course of action, to choose between alternatives and is not compelled to act contrary to his choice or prevented from acting according to his choice. This kind of freedom is sometimes called 'negative freedom' or 'freedom from' as contrasted with 'freedom to'. Now, if freedom means the right of individual choice between alternatives, this implies that the alternatives are or can be known to the individual who chooses; that an opportunity is given to the individual to understand the character of available alternatives and that he is in a position to make a deliberate and informed choice. An example of this may be taken from my work in College. I am offered academic freedom, freedom of thought which I can express to students by choosing the content of my lectures and their presentation. I am free from coercion and constraint. Now this is not absolute freedom because I am still bound by the syllabus of the college which is designed to cover ground deemed most valuable to the students as future teachers. But I am still free to interpret the syllabus in my own way. My freedom entails all sorts of responsibility — to make sure that students are well prepared for their finals, to avoid presenting biased views by which they may or may not be unduly influenced. A large part of my work is an attempt to encourage students to think, not simply to assimilate my opinions. One way of achieving this is to expose them to as many different views as possible.

Truth has a better chance of emerging if people are allowed to voice their opinions. If established opinions are true or right then they will only be strengthened by being challenged, if false or wrong, their falsity will be exposed. This challenging of views is in an important way essential for arriving at the truth. Children sometimes provide such a challenge stemming from their particular viewpoint which we, as grown ups, are no longer capable of being aware of until it is pointed out by a child, sometimes with devastating effect! But at the same time it must be remembered that a child does not possess the breadth of knowledge which allows his choices to be informed and thus we have no right to impose the enormous responsibility of choosing his education, his way of being educated, on the child. This would in fact be a gross interference with his freedom. I shall elaborate on this presently.

So far we have been discussing 'freedom from'. In addition to that notion, we also make claims about 'freedom to' or 'freedom for'. The latter are aspects of positive freedom. This kind of freedom is closely connected with political and social issues and in that context it is almost invariably a demand for a particular liberty, a demand in respect of some freedom *for* or *in* the exercise of a particular activity. These interests or activities are usually taken as possessing some special moral and/or social importance. The positive aspect of freedom shows in an important way that Mill's definition of freedom as an absence of constraint or coercion is too limited a conception. Mill's conception is an abstract one, a conception of freedom which covers many species, but deals only with the abstract and indeterminate possibility of choice. Positive notions of freedom, on the other hand, attempt to identify specific spheres of human activity — freedom of thought and speech, freedom of worship, of movement, of assembly and association, freedom of use and disposal of one's property, freedom in the choice of jobs and so on. All these imply the absence of coercion or interference, i.e. negative notions concerned with an abstract or indirect idea of free choice but in addition they stress specific kinds of human activity. I say, they *imply* the absence of coercion or interference because the two notions of freedom are, I think, *logically linked*. If something constrains and thus prevents me *from* doing what I wish to do then it follows that I am in fact not *free to* do it. Conversely, if I am *free to* do a certain action it is because nothing prevents or constrains me *from* doing it. Thus if I demand freedom from some specific constraint, unless my demand is closely linked with a specific wish to do something in particular, then my demand or the rationality of that demand may be questioned. Given, as I suggested, that there is a logical link between negative and positive notions of freedom, I still think that the distinction is a helpful one. The distinction focuses our attention on what we are demanding in a particular case, what is sought. This enables us to make judgments as to the rationality of our demands. Our demand for a particular freedom from. . . gets spelled out more clearly, is more completely expressed if we follow it by stating why we make this demand — we demand freedom from. . . because it will allow us freedom to. . . . Positive freedoms focus on specific spheres of individual and social activity and enable us to 'come down to cases' in order to examine what is involved. Now, when a child makes a choice it is usually to do x rather than y. This happens within a set social framework of the classroom. Classes are usually divided into working groups in most modern schools. The first consideration here is non-interference and no coercion to be exercised by one group over any other. Democratic decisions can, to a significant degree, be taken by the children themselves, to what degree, will depend on their age. But what must here be remembered is that the range of alternatives will of necessity be restricted because the children will be ignorant of certain possible alternatives and also because children cannot, in many cases, see the value of certain activities such as reading or writing and may, therefore, not choose them for themselves. This is why a teacher must to a certain extent limit and control their choices. How this is done and to what extent it is justified cannot be stated *a priori* for all cases. Each case has to be decided individually, according to what is involved. Now, at first glance, one's reaction may be — well, in that case the children are not free, they are coerced or manipulated by the teacher. It is here that, I think, we are most in danger of being led astray by our thinking. Manipulation and coercion implies, at least partly, a purposeful concealment of alternatives. This, it seems to me, no teacher can be accused of without very good grounds for such an accusation. A teacher's role, as I see it, is constantly to make his pupils aware of as many alternatives as possible but these cannot be revealed chaotically, without some kind of structuring on the part of the teacher. The nature of knowledge is such that there exist logical connections within areas of knowledge and also logical sequences or priorities. What I mean here is that a child must understand certain things before he can proceed to understand others. One of the most important decisions a teacher has to take is how best to present a subject which his pupils will be learning. Since much learning is a matter of experience, one way of presenting a subject is by enabling children to proceed from the concrete and the particular to the abstract and the general. This is because the concrete and the particular taught can be brought into the child's experience by the teacher. While a teacher may be aware of these issues there is yet another important aspect which needs to be stressed. In order to give a child the necessary conditions in which he is put in a position to make free, responsible choices, the teacher has to provide what Mill calls 'a variety of conditions', conditions where the child hears a variety of views, beliefs and facts expressed, where there is considerable opportunity provided for various tastes, pursuits, interests, abilities and codes of conduct. These opportunities provide the basis for the development of a child's ability to make rational judgments. It is a part, if not the most important part, of a teacher's work to cultivate in the children a recognition of the importance of rational judgments and rational thinking. But the development of rational thinking and rational judgments has to have a basis. It is not always appropriate to reason with children, children whose powers in that direction are not yet developed; children have to learn to be choosers. My point can, perhaps, be put more clearly by quoting from Rousseau:

> 'Reason with children' was Locke's chief maxim; it is in the height of fashion at present, and I hardly think it is justified by its results; those children who have been constantly reasoned with strike me as exceptionally silly. Of all human faculties reason . . . is the last and choicest growth – and you would use this for the child's early training? To make a man reasonable is the coping stone of a good education, and yet you profess to train a child through his reason. You begin at the wrong end (Rousseau, 1966 ed., p. 53).

This quotation implies that one should never reason with young children and this, I think, would be wrong but it serves very well to emphasise the importance of what a teacher should put in the way of his pupils and it also focuses our attention on the fact that children, while learning, are developing their powers of choice, they are not yet free to exercise them fully. A good teacher, it seems to me, is aware of a child's limitations in this respect.

Finally, I should like to draw attention to another aspect of freedom which has to be afforded to the child – this is his undisputed right not to be ignored or, as often happens between adults and children, patronised or despised. In other words, his freedom as a person, as a particular individual, has to be respected, his uniqueness must be sufficiently recognised and catered for. A child must never be treated as a unit, as a statistical or social unit whose specific personal features and purposes are ignored.

In summary, I have spoken of two different kinds of determinism and we have seen that not all versions of this theory are in opposition to the possibility of freedom.

I also tried to show that there are different kinds of freedom and that the notion of freedom involves a negative and a positive element; the negative referring to the absence of interference, coercion, undue control or obstruction, the positive side being concerned with the processes of choosing and freedom to act on one's own initiative and the opportunity to pursue various specific human activities. But the choice has to be a responsible one in the sense that it is informed and rational. A part of what is involved here is that freedom also demands self-discipline which will govern our choices. Thus we could see the process of educating as a process leading to freedom, enabling man to be a chooser, a rational being whose choices are not closed up by ignorance or inability to reason adequately. Therefore a teacher's task here is not so much concerned with giving complete freedom of action to the child (since this is a rather empty notion) as with providing the necessary background in order to put the child in a position in which he can make truly free choices — free because responsible and informed. How well informed these choices will be is to a large extent, although not exclusively, up to the teacher.

It is essential when deciding on a course of action not to confuse these different kinds of freedom as this will enable the teacher to see any problem arising in a positive and constructive way. I said just now that how well choices will be informed is to a large extent, though not exclusively, up to the teacher. I mean here important social considerations which often enter into play in a way which positively limits the kind of development we have been discussing. A good example of this is given by J. Klein (1965). She tries to list certain abilities which are presupposed in a person who qualifies as a chooser. These are: the ability to abstract and use generalizations, the ability to perceive the world as an ordered universe, the ability to plan ahead and the ability to exercise self-control. She uses the researches of Bernstein and Luria to show that the extent to which these various abilities will develop depends on the prevalence of an elaborated code of language which only operates in some sections of society as opposed to a restricted code to be found in other sections of society. She also stresses the point that certain beliefs, conduct and preferences of some working-class families are reflected in the upbringing of their children in that the future as such has a limited relevance to them; they suffer from prejudices, preconceptions and unthinking acceptances of all sorts of beliefs from colour prejudice to a blind acceptance of the merits of, say, advertised products. The teacher's task is to combat this both by cultivating what Bernstein calls the elaborated code of language and, through it, to develop the capacity for rational judgments and a willingness to think for oneself.

But what of the teacher's freedom? I have here been suggesting what amounts to rules which the teacher has to follow in order to provide for the pupil's freedom. Well, this is only another instance which shows the necessity of rules if we are to have freedom and the responsibility it brings in its wake. The teacher's freedom to teach imposes on him certain restrictions such as I have already mentioned. Freedom inevitably brings responsibility. This is why certain progressive schools which pride themselves on having no rules at all fill me with apprehension. The rationale behind this system of education is that it is supposed to encourage children 'to stand on their own two feet' and to develop their independence. One might ask here: independence from what? Surely not from other members of society! Such a view, apart from ignoring the dangers of indiscriminate bullying and such like, also ignores another very important consideration — a curtailment of freedom from want. The children are not free from want, their being kept in ignorance of rules of social behaviour is a want, a lack. They are, further, coerced into making choices which they are not in a position to make freely for the reasons already given. As I have tried to argue, the search for grounds and reasons for one's choice is at the very heart of a truly free person. The question 'What ought I to do?', implies alternatives which the person making the choice weighs up rationally. If no such grounds are provided then the child is in a state of confusion and likely to go for any suggestion offered. This is very akin to the notion of brainwashing where the technique is (in very simplified terms) to achieve a state of utter confusion in the victim who is then ready, indeed grateful, to grasp at any coherent idea suggested to him, an idea or course of action which would under normal conditions be totally unacceptable to him. In brainwashing the technique is designed to put the victim in a state in which he is precisely unable to make a rational or, for that matter, any kind of choice. A part of what is involved in our form of life, because of the sort of creatures we are, is that we become badly confused and cannot pursue our lives free from intolerable pressures unless some conditions of order are provided. Our very reasoning depends on our relying on the fact that we live in an ordered and fairly predictable universe. This also applies to certain basic moral rules which all of us agree to uphold, rules such as those about stealing, murder, respect for persons, etc. Whatever our personal opinions, they develop out of a common framework which we all share and agree upon. It is only from an ordered basis that we are in a position to demand changes. Coherence is essential not only for rationality but for a feeling of security for which grown-ups and children alike have a basic need.

Further reading

The texts in the bibliography provide a comprehensive discussion on the topic of man's freedom. For further reading related to politics and education the following are relevant: G. H. Bantock, *Freedom and Authority in Education*, Faber, 1965; S. I. Benn and R. S. Peters, *Social Principles and the Democratic State*, Allen & Unwin, 1965; I. Berlin, *Two Concepts of Liberty*, Clarendon Press, 1958; M. Cranston, *Freedom: A New Analysis*, Longman, 1967.

Bibliography

KLEIN, J. (1965), *Samples of English Culture*, Routledge & Kegan Paul, 2 vols.
MILL, J. S. (1859), *On Liberty*, London (World Classic Series, Oxford University Press, 1912).
REID, THOMAS, (1969 ed.), *Essays on the Active Powers of Man*, MIT Press.
ROUSSEAU, J.-J. (1966 ed.), *Emile*, New York Everyman's Library, Dent.
TAYLOR, R. (1967), 'Determinism', in *Encyclopaedia of Philosophy*, Macmillan.

Chapter eleven

Authority

D.H. Cleife

There are what appear to be two contradictory demands about behaviour made at present by those in industry, in government and in
society at large. These are a demand for greater freedom and a demand
for an increase in authority; a demand for liberty and a demand for law
and order; a demand to be allowed to express one's views and a demand
to be told what to do. Authority is seen by some to be desirable and by
others only fit to be ignored· or even to be removed. This is also true in
education.

In education, authority is often associated with dogmatism and re-
pression, supported by threat, deprivation of privilege, punishment or
expulsion. In its place is advocated a greater freedom for expression and
decision. Teachers, students and children should make decisions on
matters such as the organisation of halls of residence, the content of the
curriculum and issues of discipline. This is a participation in governing.
What is also expressed is the view that authority is wrong in principle. It
is regarded as inhuman and insensitive. The reason for the adoption of
such an attitude may be easily understood, but the view as it stands will
not hold much water.

What appears puzzling about all those who oppose the existence of
authority is that when it comes to decisions concerning the diagnosis of
appendicitis, or carburettor failure, they leave these matters to the
experts in medicine and automobile engineering. They readily accept
this authority. They speak proudly of an acquaintance who 'knows his
job' and will recommend someone who 'has it at his fingertips'.

There is obviously a problem here. Is authority a good or a bad
thing? A solution is offered in the section below on the nature of
authority. Briefly it will be argued that the solution is this. While such
dissenters may speak as if they want to get rid of authority altogether,
they cannot mean that at all. In fact, authority, I shall claim, cannot be
dispensed with. It is here to stay and its place here is logical in character
and so will withstand any attacks whatever. This view may be

immediately regarded as supporting 'the establishment' — buttressing the crumbling bourgeoisie.

Against this charge, however, I shall argue that my case for the necessity of authority is a case that leaves plenty of room for rational questioning about *who* is to exercise authority and *how*. It will allow for people's questioning authority in all sections of society, government and governed, employers and employees, educators and educated. For the disagreement is over who has the right to exercise authority rather than with authority itself. The dispute concerns the proper conferring of authority on someone. What can never be a proper subject for dispute is 'authority' itself; this now has to be shown.

The nature of authority

The first point to be made about authority is that it is vested in someone or some body of people. It may be in a king, an umpire, a general or a committee. Often such authority changes hands. In the past, in Western civilisation, absolute authority was attributed by Divine Right to kings, but over the years this has changed and today it is generally given to governments. This gradual shift of authority from individuals to bodies has had its impact on education too. But of course the question of what authority is, is quite separate from *who* has authority and whether he should possess it.

Now we come to the heart of the matter. The idea of authority exists because of one simple but important fact, namely, that in any society some people know more than others. In any situation where one person is ignorant and another has knowledge of something, the one who *knows* is, in a minimal sense, an authority. A fitter and turner knows better than his apprentice; the coach than his pupil; the instructor than the learner driver. But why does this happen?

Well, in any society whatever there will be those, usually the older people, who have acquired certain information about their past and their surroundings, and who can perform all manner of skills. In primitive societies the men know how and what to hunt. They teach their sons, who in turn will pass this on to their own children. They have a knowledge and an understanding of their environment. They possess a degree of expertise and skill. Anyone who does not possess such understanding or ability will obviously consult those who do. It is these people who know, who will be placed in positions of authority. By the nature of their expertise and ability they will teach as well as judge and in more civilised societies forms of assessment are employed to establish the possession of such competences.

Of course, there are people in positions of authority who are there because of *who* they know rather than *what* they know. We could all cite examples of teachers, for instance, who are inefficient. But the fact that there are such cases does not entitle us to say that we just happen to be *lucky* if those in authority are also good at their job. In general this must be true, for any institution will break down unless it has respect for efficiency and standards.

Let us put this argument more formally. In any society there will be correct ways of saying and doing things, in a very general sense — there will be rules — and in a human society where some are born before others, and have had an opportunity to learn — unlike a society of angels — some will understand the rules better than others. In fact, whenever a rule can be followed it can also be broken.

Another important consideration in this argument, which is pertinent to teaching, is the fact that a person cannot learn these rules for himself. Putting it more bluntly, no one can literally say, with regard to rules, that he is 'self-taught'. They belong, both in language and behaviour, to the institution of home or school. They have arisen over a long period and it takes experience to acquire them. But the more important point is not that it would be just time-consuming to acquire these rules without teaching but that it would be impossible since our physical world and our relationships with one another can be interpreted in a variety of ways (see chapter 3).

Authority and education

It has been argued in the previous section that the concept of authority is really of two kinds. To possess knowledge and expertise is to be *an* authority, and since such people generally are in positions where they can exercise their abilities, we speak of them as being *in* authority. It is the first meaning which is the more important. Let us now turn to education with this distinction in mind.

In education we speak of someone being an authority in a subject or a group of subjects and we look to him for guidance and advice and occasionally to settle disputes about some fact, school organisation or method of teaching. For example, we speak of someone being an authority in music, vertical grouping or programmed learning. That is exactly comparable to the situation outside education, say as in engineering or law.

In education not anyone can be a teacher, not anyone can be placed in a position to exercise the authority expected of a teacher. So some kind of test of competence and assessment of ability must be made to guarantee that the person is fit for his position and can make good use of it. If teaching were a 'free for all' the schools and other institutions of education would become a jungle of incompetences. No, the vetting of people is an essential and necessary part of the profession.

It would be misleading, though, to present a picture of children fully aware of the competence of their teachers and eagerly consulting them; for children in this country and most other countries are compelled by law to attend school. Furthermore, even if they were not made to go, they would not be in a position to judge whether they wished to take advice from an expert in education. In fact, the purpose of education is largely to enable children to come to recognise and possess desirable human abilities. So education is in a different position from other professions. In education children are often unable to recognise grounds for the authority of their teacher. How then is this obstacle overcome? Although it sounds somewhat fierce the word we use for the means by which this authority is exercised is power. The word may call up associations with brutal methods employed to bring subjects to heel and in education the word of late has been used in such strongly emotive phrases as 'student power' and 'pupil power'.

Some philosophers have claimed that authority is the exercising of legitimate power, and that this allows the use of force in order to compel those being ruled to conform to the law. But as teachers we cannot leave it at this because some of the coercive forces used by those in authority in some societies are totally unacceptable in education. Reference is being made here not only to punitive methods used such as the use of sanctions and curfews, etc., but also to the more subtle methods such as indoctrination, propaganda, brainwashing and conditioning.

Now, if we accept that authority is a kind of power backed when necessary by force, this does not imply that rational men have chosen to submit to an authority that uses the kinds of coercive procedures indicated above. For surely the functions of those who have been placed in positions of authority are, first, to regulate behaviour wherever possible without the use of force and, second, if required to use force, to make clear what measures are being taken and why. (By 'force' is meant compulsion by the use of punishment.) Regulating behaviour must be the teacher's main concern in exercising his authority and it will demand from him skill and imagination. The kind of skill necessary will be discussed later. But the over-riding consideration of all in education, administrators and teachers alike, must be that if authority breaks down and those in authority lose the control and the co-operation of their pupils they may have to resort to the use of appropriate force, i.e. punishment, in order to maintain standards of behaviour that are necessary so that education can take place.

The question now arises, what kind of force or punishment should be used in schools when authority breaks down — as it often does. In considering this question we must, as teachers, immediately reject the 'retributive' form of punishment for this would be an act of vengeance (e.g. pinch for pinch, kick for kick), an act hardly suitable for children of any age. Likewise it seems to me unjust and unimaginative on the teacher's part to punish one child or group of children in the hope that it may deter others from committing some similar offence.

However, a more positive approach to the use of punishment in education can be taken by looking at the school's function as an agent of socialisation. This process of socialising is not a matter only of teaching social and moral knowledge and skills but of reforming behaviour that is not acceptable to the community. In this case it is more imaginative to think of punishment in schools as reformative in nature; this means that teachers, in exercising their authority, should lead children towards an understanding of the rules of society and their own school rules. Also a sense of obligation must be engendered in children and the kinds of feeling characteristic of mature and rational human beings; feelings such as compassion, sympathy, respect for rules and other people, shame when they commit serious offences themselves, and shock when they see the result of someone else's evil act. Experienced teachers will know that these desirable feelings are not easy to foster, especially in those children who have been deprived of a satisfactory social and moral climate at home.

The type of control an individual teacher exercises over his children in socialising them will, of course, depend upon many things. It will depend upon what kind of person he is — his beliefs and home background — and his knowledge of children and how they learn and develop in all fields. It will depend too upon his own education and probably, most important of all, his knowledge of himself. This is important because if teachers are to use their authority sensibly in schools they must be able to analyse the teaching situation in which they still are, in my opinion, by far the most important factor.

But being able, as part of self-knowledge, to assess accurately one's own behaviour as a variable in the learning situation is not easy. Help can be obtained by studying the findings of researches carried out by social psychologists on the relationship of teachers to their pupils and the effect that this has upon the social climate of the group. The now long-standing but none the less very respected research of Lippit and White (1943) has revealed three broad types of relationship that can exist between teachers and their pupils. These are (i) authoritarian, (ii) *laissez-faire*, and (iii) democratic. It is claimed in these researches that each type of relationship leads to a different social climate within the classroom and by coming to understand these relationships and their social effect teachers can help themselves to assess their own influence upon a group of children no matter what the teaching situation may be.

An 'authoritarian' teacher is described as one who firmly controls his pupils by initiating and organising everything that goes on in the classroom. He is impersonal and his main methods of control are to praise, blame and punish. If one observes a teacher working over a long period in this way it is obvious that he is imposing upon his pupils his own pattern of thinking and knowledge. It is claimed that as a result those subjected to this kind of control become passive absorbers of instruction and information.

A '*laissez-faire*' teacher, it is stated by these researchers, will be the converse of this. He will purposely withdraw completely from any position of authority and will go to great lengths in order not to influence his pupils' behaviour or thinking in any way. He neither leads nor controls his children and although he is present to answer their questions his policy is to leave children to their own devices. The children will decide what they want to do and how to do it. Teachers who use this method are hesitant to exert any pressure on the child, either mental or physical, and would never use force in order to maintain order no matter what the situation might be in the classroom. Researches carried out with older pupils in this situation show that this method leads to insecurity — pupils, lacking the initiative to solve their own problems, contrary to what is anticipated by advocates of this policy, ask repeatedly for help.

A 'democratic' teacher, it is stated, plays the role of group leader. His main objective is to lead his children in the study of problems relevant to the knowledge he wants them to learn. This method presupposes respect for one another's ideas whether they come from the teacher or from the group. In this situation, it is claimed by researchers, children are encouraged through hinting, prompting and guiding to think for themselves.

Here the teacher is no less in authority than the 'authoritarian' and '*laissez-faire*' teacher, in that he is responsible for his pupils, for their learning and welfare. He differs from them in the way his authority is manifested. That is, he is authoritative without being authoritarian. The research then brings out clearly how differently authority can be exercised. However, what form of authority a teacher adopts should be governed by his educational aims.

The teacher as an authority

It was stated above that exercising authority in school demands much skill and imagination on the teacher's part; but what skill? and how is a teacher to obtain this skill? and how is he to develop his imagination in this area?

To answer these questions it will be convenient to consider briefly two aspects of education to bring out more clearly what is meant here by a teacher's being an authority in education. First, one can look at its factual aspect referred to in future as A. This is a composite body of knowledge contributed to by psychologists, sociologists, anthropologists, philosophers and scholars in their attempt to explain human behaviour and to indicate what people should learn. Second, there is the active aspect of education (B) in which teachers endeavour to make use of the knowledge in A, to develop objectives for and methods of teaching. This means that B is based upon and follows a set of recommendations (formulated in A) regarding the content of what is taught and the manner of teaching it. The efficacy of these methods and the value of what is taught will depend *first* upon the relevance to education of the work that makes up A — the psychology and sociology, etc. — and *second* upon the efficiency with which this work is *interpreted* by teachers and administrators and then *used* by them. This last point emphasises a vital issue in education — the relationship between theory and practice. If theory is to illuminate practice it should arise from practice in the classroom and not from clinics or the study of the behaviour of cats and rats. That said, how are teachers to make up their minds about their aims and methods, i.e. how are they to interpret, evaluate and use the knowledge contained in A? Teachers are bombarded with ideas and recommendations from popular educational literature. Many of these ideas are very obscure and teachers will need to have a good understanding of the recommendations that come from A before they can make judgments on them. This point can be made clearer by considering a few important words and ideas that have 'popped up' from time to time, and try to determine their meaning from their use in educational literature — 'integrated day', 'core curriculum', 'on-going process', 'growth', 'need' and so on. The real questions to ask at this point are: have teachers and administrators made up their minds about what these important terms mean? Can they use them clearly to express their aims in education or in discussing their work with one another? This is doubtful but it is an important part of a teacher's function as an authority on education to give some thought to these ideas and find time to discuss them along with others that arise from considering the work in A with their colleagues. It is surprising how little of this is done in most schools. If everyone concerned with and interested in education were to do this seriously it is highly probable that more effective communication between individuals about matters vital in education would exist. This would without doubt be of benefit to those endeavouring to relate theory to practice, and could lead to more purposeful work being done in schools of all types.

Conclusion

Having examined the notion of a teacher's being *in* authority and being *an* authority we can now bring the two together and show how they must be seen as complementary. For one without the other will not lead to effective teaching. A teacher in authority only, in control only, need not necessarily be teaching — he can be child-minding and seeing that the children obey the school rules. This will be like carrying out an extended playtime duty in a traditional school. Conversely a teacher who is an authority in a subject but not in control of the teaching situation will likewise not be teaching — his efforts to pass on information will be wasted if his pupils do not attend to him or respect him. It follows then that if the teacher is to educate he must be both in authority and an authority in the disciplines relevant to education and in some area of academic knowledge. This does not mean that all teachers should be educational psychologists but it does mean that they should strive to reach the position where they are able to evaluate methods of teaching and then choose those that help their pupils to become progressively more aware of what is happening to them. The authoritarian teacher in approaching his work does not apparently display sufficient awareness of how children learn. His only interest is in passing on information and his audience remains passive. Conversely, the *laissez-faire* teacher, it is claimed, displays little concern for the passing on of knowledge; he concentrates too much upon keeping children busy by allowing them to follow their own interests. Now the teacher using his authority rationally would attempt to strike a balance between these two approaches. He would show respect for the child but would not accede to the child's every wish. Unlike the authoritarian teacher he would allow the child much freedom to question but he would, through prompting, hinting, suggesting and demonstrating, etc., lead the child towards acquiring, with understanding, valued knowledge and skills in the most *economical* way. For children have much to learn in the short time that they are with teachers in school and it would be impossible for them to discover for themselves all that they need to know in order to become mature and rational human beings. Therefore, as has been argued throughout, teachers must use their authority with good reason if children are to be educated by them rather than just trained to carry out some specific task in society or left to their own devices. This means that through skilful handling by teachers in authority pupils should eventually become responsible for organising their own learning and they should come to see the reason for much of what they learn. In this way they will be moving towards becoming authorities themselves in some area of knowledge. We have now returned full circle and can bring in the question we began with. How does the pupil exercise authority? How much authority, for example, should be delegated to senior pupils in schools so that they can have some say in their own education? In answering this question two important principles must be considered. First, the principle of academic freedom. A teacher as an authority in some area of knowledge must have the freedom to choose what he thinks is best for his pupils to learn. He must not be inhibited by those who have not yet acquired his expertise. Neither should he be inhibited by the views of politicians, economists or other administrators who will see education as an instrument which can be designed to suit the particular end that they have in mind. This end is usually an instrumental one, which means that they expect pupils to be trained for specific places and tasks in society. It would, on the other hand, be wrong for him to ignore them. Second, teachers must have sole responsibility for constructing syllabuses and for selecting pupils for courses and for examining them where necessary. They should also have sole responsibility for appointing colleagues whom they consider suitable to help them with this work. However, there are many areas where it would be wise for teachers, especially in secondary and higher education, to consult their pupils — for instance, pupils may have a valuable contribution to make to any discussion on methods of teaching and methods of examining. But it must be repeated that teachers should decide what is to be taught and what is to be examined. It is by virtue of his ability that he has been placed in this position where he must take *final* responsibility for the learning of his pupils. Social control in the school is also an area in which pupils can participate. The prefect system is not being advocated here but senior pupils should most certainly be consulted on any matters of discipline and organisation within the school. They should help to formulate school rules and to decide courses of action that could lead to better relationships amongst parents, staff and pupils, for here it may be felt that teachers and pupils are equal in their capacity to make right decisions.

From these points then it can be seen that in using their authority rationally teachers will involve their pupils in making many decisions that have traditionally been left to headmasters and staffs of schools alone. But in doing so they must not put in jeopardy learning and the passing on of knowledge to those who are to follow them.

Further reading

A more extensive treatment of 'Authority' can be found in *Social Principles and the Democratic State*, ed. S. I. Benn and R. S. Peters, Allen & Unwin, 1959, ch. 14 and a symposium contributed to by R. S. Peters and P. G. Winch in *Political Philosophy*, ed. A. Quinton, Oxford University Press, 1967.

G. H. Bantock who takes what might be called a conservative view of authority applies it to education in *Freedom and Authority in Education*, Faber, 1959.

Examples of a progressive approach to authority are in plenty in R. Skidelsky's interesting book, *English Progressive Schools*, Penguin, 1959.

Bibliography

LIPPIT, R. and WHITE, R. K. (1943), 'The Social Climate of Children's Groups', in Barker, R. G., *et al.* (eds), *Child Behavior and Development*, McGraw-Hill.